M000191127

COPING WITH KIDS AND SCHOOL

A GUIDE FOR PARENTS

Linda Albert, Ph.D.

E. P. DUTTON, INC.   NEW YORK

Published in the United States by E. P. Dutton, Inc.
2 Park Avenue, New York, N.Y. 10016

Library of Congress Cataloging in Publication Data

Albert, Linda.
    Coping with kids and school.

    Bibliography: p.
    1. Home and school.   2. Parent and child.   I. Title.
LC225.A58   1984   370.19'31   84-8071
ISBN: 0-525-24251-1

Published simultaneously in Canada by
Fitzhenry and Whiteside, Limited, Toronto

WORLD

10 9 8 7 6 5 4 3 2 1

First Edition

To my father

Contents

Acknowledgments

There are many people I want to thank for their help in creating this book.

First there is my family, which believes in me, shares my excitement when the writing is going well, and offers strong support when the flow of words is blocked and progress is stalled. I am lucky to have the encouragement of my children, Ken Moraff, Judith M. Rachel, and Steve Moraff; my father, J. Louis Albert, and stepmother, Dori; my brother Neale Albert and his wife Margaret; and my wonderful aunt, Florence Kreisler.

Equally important are the close friends who are always there for whatever is needed at the moment. Fern Chapin's daily telephone calls provided just the right mixture of distraction and support. Elaine Shimberg offered the advice and understanding only a writer can give to another writer. Mark Stuart convinced me "I could" when I felt like "I couldn't."

For my understanding of kids, parents, and teachers I am once again indebted to the theories and methods which were originally developed by Alfred Adler and Rudolf Dreikurs, and expanded upon by my friends and colleagues in the North American Society of Adlerian Psychology. My hope is that I have added to and organized these ideas in a meaningful way that will be helpful to all of us.

I'd also like to acknowledge Daniel Eckstein and my colleagues at Lyons International University where this manuscript was submitted as part of the requirement for my doctoral degree.

Thanks are also due to the great numbers of children who called me "teacher" during my years with the public schools in Ithaca, New York. They taught me at least as much as I taught them. It is really for kids that this book is written. They are the ones who will benefit most when their parents learn how to cope with schools.

Before this manuscript reached its final form, a number of colleagues offered their time and expertise by reading the original draft and offering suggestions. Thank you Carol Arnold, Nancy Berla, Lynn Bounds, Mary Bullerman, Linda Delapenha, and Joan Herndon.

Thanks also to Diane Harris, senior editor at E. P. Dutton, who saw the need for a book such as this, asked me to write it, and then provided the support and professional expertise necessary to accomplish the task.

The questions which appear in this book are the real words of real parents. Some of the questions were asked in person by parents after hearing me speak at workshops and conventions; others were sent to me by readers of the "Coping with Kids" newspaper column. Thank you all for asking. I hope the answers provide you with the information and encouragement you need to help your kids succeed in school.

LINDA ALBERT
Tampa, Florida
March 1984

1

●●●●●●●●●●●●●●●●●●●●●●●●●●●●●●●●●●●

The Search
for Excellence

Parents can make a difference. Don't waste time wondering if it's OK to get involved in your kids' school life. If you take an active part in your kids' education, their chances to succeed in school increase dramatically. I've never yet met parents who didn't want the years in school to be successful for their kids. Yet few moms and dads are sure about which parental attitudes and actions will foster such success.

In 1981, the National Committee for Citizens in Education published an annotated bibliography entitled "Parent Participation—Student Achievement, The Evidence Grows," citing twenty-six separate research studies that show the positive effect parents' involvement has on their kids' learning. What we've been lacking is a realistic and informative manual for parents that makes clear just which skills, strategies, and infor-

1

mation parents need to cope with kids and schools. The purpose of this book is to fill that gap. Let's begin our search for excellence by adopting a positive attitude towards schools.

The Good News

On Sunday, January 1, 1984, *Parade* magazine published a four-page story entitled "The Good News About Our Public Schools." The writer told how in 1983 the Ford Foundation had singled out ninety-two successful high schools in twenty large cities and rewarded them with praise and $1000 incentive awards. And in his book *Making Schools Work,* Robert Benjamin describes in exciting terms a number of successful elementary schools in various kinds of neighborhoods around the country. Among the schools cited were:

• Shaker Heights High in Shaker Heights, Ohio, a school where 38% of the students belong to minority groups and 82% of the graduating seniors enter four-year college programs.

• The elementary schools in Mt. Vernon, New York, where 37% of the third graders used to fail state competency exams in reading and math. By 1980, only 6% of the students failed these exams. At the sixth-grade level, the failure rate dropped from 50% to 25%.

• The schools in the Lake Washington school district in Kirkland, Washington, where students' basic skills scores rose 30% in the last five years.

Many more books could be written (and perhaps should be written) about the successes many schools are experiencing today.

Unfortunately, what isn't working usually gets more media coverage than what is working. 1983 was the year of the alarming national reports on the declining quality of American education. Articles on declining test scores, increasing dropout rates, lack of discipline in the classroom, and poorly qualified teachers appear regularly in the papers. There's no doubt that our elementary and secondary school systems have much room for improvement. Perhaps all the negative attention from the press has accomplished one important task— plans for upgrading education at all levels are being devised by parents, educators and politicians alike and are beginning to be implemented in many of our schools. Here are just a few of the positive changes already under way:

New teaching methods have enabled many schools to reverse declining achievement levels. "Mastery learning," a method that emphasizes teaching in small steps and testing kids to make sure they have learned each step before they progress, is being used by many schools, particularly in reading instruction. Also, technology is changing teaching methods by introducing computers and computer-aided instruction into the curriculum. While teaching with computers is too recent an innovation to have been systematically evaluated, there are countless possibilities for successful use of computers in the classroom.

The proliferation of programs for kids with special needs is another promising trend. These programs stem from the realization that children have different needs and abilities, rates of learning, and styles of learning. We have programs for the handicapped, for the gifted, for those for whom English is a second language. We have remedial reading and remedial math programs. And there are entire alternative school programs. Some schools emphasize basic skills, others focus on multi-cultural learning, and still others emphasize math, science, and computer studies.

Opportunities for parents to participate in school decision-making are expanding. One area where parents often have a strong voice is in the special programs mentioned above. And programs that are federally mandated frequently require a parent advisory council that makes recommendations and oversees the operation of the program on a local school level. Also, local PTAs, which in the past frequently confined themselves to raising money for school needs, now have local, state, and national legislative policies and actively work for needed educational changes. In fact, the local PTA is often the best starting point for individual parents who want to initiate changes. Another promising new trend, called school-based management, gives more decision-making power to the administrators of local schools. When decisions are made at this level, administrators can be more responsive to the needs and wishes of local parents.

Another promising innovation is that many industries are becoming partners in education with the schools in their area. Some companies provide speakers that introduce kids to their particular business, invite the kids to see their business operation firsthand and even provide a school-supervised work-study experience. Others, like IBM and Apple, provide direct services to schools by donating new or used equipment, and occasionally even providing personnel on a limited basis to teach the kids how to use it. Innisbrook Resort in Tarpon Springs, Florida, assists the local elementary school. During the past couple of years, Innisbrook has provided buses for field trips and lent the use of its print shop to publish a book of poetry written by the children. It has established the "Teacher of the Month Award" for which it donates a prize of a free Sunday brunch for two at one of the resort's restaurants. And it allows employees one hour a week of released time to tutor kids in the school. Businesses taking part in the "Adopt-a-School" program in Dallas, Texas, donated more than two million dollars in goods and services during the 1980–81 school year.

While we applaud such changes and innovations, many will not bear fruit for many years to come. We need to take action now to help our kids succeed today. Don't let negative reports about schools discourage you from actively participating in your kids' education. Keep the good news in mind.

Specific Skills and Strategies

In a recent survey funded by the Charles F. Kettering Foundation, three out of four parents felt they lacked the skills needed to become involved in their kids' schooling. Yet there is nothing mysterious about these skills—they just need to be identified and described in order for parents to use them.

In the pages that follow, you will learn more about the communication skills needed to establish and maintain effective relationships with your children's teachers; procedures for contacting teachers, preparing for conferences, and sharing information about your children; and suggestions for handling difficult situations that might lead to communication breakdowns between parents and teachers.

If your children are experiencing either academic or behavior problems in school this book will give you step-by-step procedures so that you can identify the causes of those difficulties and then devise the best strategy to alleviate them.

Sometimes situations arise between kids and teachers or kids and parents that require the use of negotiation and conflict resolution skills. Perhaps your child doesn't seem to be able to get along with his teacher and comes home tearful and angry every day. Maybe there are power struggles at home each evening over homework. Using the right tools to solve such problems will make everyone's life more pleasant and will help redirect your child's energies back to where they belong—on achieving excellence in school.

Meet the Specialists

At some point in your search for excellence in education you will meet the school specialists: the school nurse, counselor, psychologist, social worker, reading teacher, special education teacher, speech and language therapist, and librarian. Although not every school has all of these on staff full time, most at least have access to such professionals on a part-time basis. These specialists are on hand to provide special services for children and for their parents. You'll find one or more of them can help you if your child:

- seems upset and angry much of the time
- has a chronic health problem and needs medication during the school day
- reads at a level well below where he should
- has trouble making friends with other kids
- expresses interest in reading stories about other kids who have special family circumstances or an ethnic background like their own
- mispronounces certain letters and words.

Obviously there are many other possible problems. As you read on, you will find out more about the specialists and what they can do for you and your children. The knowledge and expertise of these specially trained professionals are some of your most valuable resources in coping with your kids and school.

More Resources for Parents

What about resources outside of school? What kinds of groups should you know about to be well-equipped to provide your child with the best opportunities? In addition to the PTA, which most parents are familiar with, there's the National Committee for Citizens in Education (NCCE). This group provides printed information on a wide variety of school-related topics such as understanding test scores and minimum competency requirements, discipline, and violence and destruction in schools. NCCE provides a telephone hotline for answering parents' questions and offers support services for initiating educational changes. The Home-School Institute, a nonprofit organization established in 1964, specializes in "nurturing the academic and social development of school-age children by involving their families in supportive activities at home." The institute provides ideas and materials for stimulating your child's intellect and for practicing academic skills at home. Also there are groups that deal with general concerns about children such as the Children's Defense Fund whose stated goal is "to ensure that every American child's basic survival needs are met." Still other groups, such as the Association for Children with Learning Disabilities, deal with specialized interests.

You'll find all these groups mentioned at various points in the book where their functions are relevant to issues being discussed. And they are also listed separately for your convenience in Appendix 3.

Since educators tell us that kids do much better in school when the discipline at home is firm, consistent, and effective, you might want to attend parenting workshops to learn more about developing improved parenting skills. You'll find lists of resources for this purpose in Appendixes 1 and 2.

School Programs and Policies

Getting better acquainted with current school programs and policies in the chapters that follow will allow you to take advantage of different options many schools offer. It's often vital to revise our ideas about schools because today's schools seem so different from those most of us knew as children. The information offered here will also help you to make sense of many of the educational reforms and changes of the last two decades. Some of the topics to be explored are:
- beginning reading programs
- all-day kindergartens for five-year-olds
- schools charging fees for programs and supplies
- rights of parents to review school records
- the contents of kids' textbooks

- computers in the classrooms
- the differences between junior high schools and middle schools.

Single parents and stepparents will be particularly interested in the information presented in Chapter 5 on how to make the schools more responsive to the needs of their children. Non-custodial parents will find tips on how they can keep involved in their children's education.

Despite the bureaucracy that surrounds our school systems, when one person joins with other like-minded individuals, he or she can accomplish a great deal towards reshaping school programs and policies. You'll find many suggestions on how to do this in the pages that follow. Getting involved in productive steps helps to dispel feelings of frustration and helplessness. United with others, you can make a difference.

Partners in Education

You, your child, and his teachers all have the same goal—the best education possible for your child. To reach that goal, working together and supporting each other's efforts is essential.

It is unfortunate that parents and teachers are not always supportive of each other. Surrounded by unpleasant statistics on an array of problems, it's human tendency, regrettable though it may be, to look for someone to blame. In the media, stories abound about parents who do a poor job of raising kids and teachers who are ill-prepared for teaching. The high visibility of an inadequate minority can make us forget that the great majority of both groups are struggling to do a responsible job of raising and educating kids.

Our tendency to blame others, to tell *them* what *they* should do differently, can give rise to a lot of mistrust, suspicion, and ill-feeling between parents and teachers. These feelings sap the motivation and energy required to take action and solve problems. The uselessness of blame is well illustrated by the story of the husband and wife who notice a snake crawling along their living room floor. Both immediately become excited, upset, and frightened. "It's your fault," screams the wife. "You left the front door open." "Nonsense," the husband replies, "It's your fault because you left the back door open." Meanwhile, because no one is focusing on solving the more immediate and important problem of removing the snake, it crawls merrily around the house at will.

It's really the kids who suffer while the adults are busy pointing fingers at each other. Kids often copy this behavior. They blame other kids, their parents, and/or their teachers, and thus avoid any constructive action of their own. To teach our children how to grow in responsibility is as important as any lesson they will learn.

Rather than blaming one another, let's acknowledge that both parents and teachers experience difficulties with kids and applaud each other's efforts to find more effective ways to parent and to teach. The large increase in both parent education and teacher in-service programs around the country bears witness to such efforts.

Don't forget that the kids are part of the team. In the past, parents and teachers could plan programs and make decisions for kids without including them in the process. No more. As John Naisbitt says so eloquently in *Megatrends*: "People whose lives are affected by a decision must be part of the process of arriving at that decision." Kids want and need to be actively involved in their education. They need to be part of the process of finding solutions where problems exist. They need to take responsibility for homework, studying for exams, achieving satisfactory grades. Ideas on how and when to involve the kids actively in their schooling are found throughout this book.

In addition, you'll learn who should take responsibility for the first steps toward solving a particular problem. You'll learn when to leave problems to the teacher and child to solve together and when to become involved yourself. When the adults work closely together as a team, it isn't possible for children to play the parent against the teacher.

How to Use This Book

This is not a book to be read once and put on the shelf. Read it through for an overview of school-related issues. Then begin following some of the hints for stimulating and motivating your kids. If your child is experiencing difficulties in school, pick one problem, read the suggested solution, and begin to deal with it. As that situation improves, start working on the next problem. Use this book as a reference for dealing with future problems whenever they arise.

To create a forum to discuss and clarify ideas before you take action, you may want to form an informal parent support group that meets regularly. This will allow you to share your successes, explore any areas where you encounter difficulty, and sharpen your understanding of the communication and conflict resolution skills suggested. You can role-play situations with teachers until you are comfortable with the steps you want to take. What's more, the combined efforts of the group members will increase the chances for success when you lobby for changes in your school. Using this book as a guide, both individual parents and parent support groups will have important background information at their disposal as well as key issues set forth in a clear and straightforward way, which will give you the tools you need to create the best possible environment for educational excellence.

2

••••••••••••••••••••••••••••••••

How to Provide an A+ Home Atmosphere

You have just returned to the kitchen after waving goodbye to your kids as they boarded the school bus. "Oh, no," you sigh, as you notice your son's geography report lying on the table just where he left it. "Not again. This is the third time this week he's forgotten something. How can I get him to remember to take his things to school?"

Unfortunately your school-related troubles aren't over for the day. When you get home from work, a note from your daughter's teacher is waiting for you. "Twice this week Betsy didn't have her math homework assignment finished. Please make sure that she completes everything tonight." You dread the struggle ahead, as you attempt to convince your daughter to complete her work.

In the middle of the struggle over homework, an encyclo-

11

pedia salesman appears at the door. He gives you a convincing line about how parents who want their kids to succeed in school must provide educational resources at home. "Is it worth the expense?" you wonder. "Why can't I just leave the job of educating my kids to the school?"

No one doubts that education begins at home, that you are your children's first teacher. How much success your child experiences in school is directly related to the quality of the learning environment you provide from birth till graduation. This quality does not depend on your socioeconomic level, age, educational attainments, or occupation; rather it's what you actually *do* with your kids that counts.

You can stimulate your children's intellect, teach them good work habits, guide their academic efforts, and motivate them to want to learn and succeed. This chapter will deal with the first three of these tasks. Providing motivation, so crucial to your children's success in school, is the subject of a chapter all its own.

Unique and Marvelous   As Pablo Casals said ". . . what do we teach our children . . . that two and two are four and that Paris is the capital of France. When will we also teach them what they are? We should say to each of them, 'Do you know what you are? You are a marvel, you are unique. In all the world, there is no other child exactly like you. . . . You have the capacity for anything. Yes, you are a marvel. . . . You must cherish one another.' "

Leave the formal teaching of academic skills to the teachers. Instead, emphasize exposure to stimulating experiences both at home and in the community. This requires a great deal of time and commitment on your part. If you're a single or working parent, finding the time may not be easy. Yet it's a mistake to rely on the schools to do these tasks for you. Teachers work with large groups of children and can't give each the individual attention that parents can. They cannot tailor activities to the needs and interests of each child. They can't provide continuity because they generally see a child for only one year. In addition, they don't carry the same weight as role models. Teachers must concentrate on teaching the basic skills while parents can focus on exploring the world with their child. A child will receive a complete education only when parents and teachers, each focused on appropriate tasks, work together.

Stimulating Your Children's Intellect

Your child's intellectual development depends heavily on the activities and experiences you provide both at home and in the community. Intellectual development is much more than learning such basic skills as reading or multiplying. It includes learning to think and speak, exploring the world, creating and enjoying art and music. When you stimulate your child in these areas, you teach your child *how* to learn and inspire him to *want* to learn. You provide the foundation for school learning.

Learning Language Skills. Help your children learn effective language skills that will build the foundation for success in reading and writing. These skills include acquiring a large vocabulary, understanding synonyms and opposites, using prepositions correctly, being familiar with the singular and plural forms of words, having the ability to categorize words, and learning proper sentence structure and grammar.

Words are the basic building blocks for successful language development. When your kids were toddlers, you probably loved teaching them the words for objects around the house. Don't stop now that they're older. All through the school years you can help to enlarge your children's vocabularies. Play games with words. An hour of Scrabble, Boggle, or Trivia can brighten a dreary, soggy Saturday afternoon. So can word puzzles of all sorts. Tell riddles and puns. Refer frequently to the dictionary and thesaurus. Study strange words that appear in stories you read aloud.

For younger children, buy or make decks of cards with pictures and words. If you and your kids play games with these cards frequently their language skills should increase dramatically. Buy the cards locally, or order them from American Guidance Service, Circle Pines, MN 55014, or from Developmental Learning Materials, 7440 Natchez Avenue, Niles, IL 60648, and ask for their catalog. Their card games for developing language skills are excellent. You'll find decks of cards that illustrate word forms such as opposites, prepositions, nouns, and verbs. Other decks illustrate categories of words that relate to food or clothing or transportation. Instructions for using these cards in creative ways come with each deck.

Think Out Loud   Share your thoughts with your kids as you go about your daily household routines. Suppose you are about to pour fabric softener into a load of wash. You might say, "Now I'll put in the softener, after the soap is finished but before the last spin. Then the clothes will feel soft and smell fresh. If I don't use softener, everyone in the family complains that the clothes are scratchy and irritating. I'll use a measuring cup to measure one-fourth of a cup, then I'll rinse it when I'm through." When kids hear you think out loud they learn to put tasks in proper sequence, to make comparisons, to see relationships, to make decisions, and to weigh alternatives. As the kids get older, you can talk about more sophisticated processes.

Make sure the kids have plenty of time to speak and to be listened to each day so that they learn to express their thoughts, ideas, and feelings with ease. To be an effective parent you'll have to do lots of listening.

Use good sentence structure and grammar so they can imitate your speech patterns. After all, that's the way they learned to speak in the first place. Avoid using baby talk and don't make fun of any grammatical mistakes your children make; undue emphasis could lead them to experience frustration or failure. Simply give them the correct words and phrases when appropriate.

Exploring the Home World. There are many home resources on which to base activities or discussions that will stimulate your children's curiosity.

A good supply of books, general magazines, and newspapers is essential, as are periodicals designed for your children's age group or specific interests. What nine-year-old could resist curling up on the couch with the latest copy of "Ranger Rick," an excellent nature magazine put out by the National Wildlife Federation? Got a kid interested in coins? You have two magazines to choose from—*COINage* or *Coins: The Magazine of Coin Collecting*. *Children's Playmate* and *Cricket Magazine* are full of stories, poems, riddles, games, craft ideas designed to keep youngsters actively involved for hours. Len Kusnetz gives you a detailed list of what's available in books and magazines in his helpful guide *Your Child can be a Super-Reader*, available from Learning House Publishers, 38 South St., Roslyn Heights, N.Y. 11576.

Are current encyclopedias in the home worth the expense? If you have easy access to a public library, perhaps not. Encyclopedias quickly become outdated. Besides, within a short time period, home computers with access to information systems will probably replace the traditional print encyclopedia. However, older, out-of-date encyclopedias can often be purchased inexpensively at flea markets and yard sales. Much of the information doesn't go out of date, such as the parts of an insect or the average daily temperature at the equator. And kids love cutting pictures from old encyclopedias to use for art projects or to illustrate reports.

TV is also an excellent educational resource when properly used. Choose programs to view as a family, making sure you take the time afterward to discuss what you saw. Munch some popcorn or snack on milk and cookies and talk about the show's characters. Did they seem real? Do people usually act this way? What would you have done in similar circumstances? Use the "w" questions—who, what, where, why. In this way you foster critical viewing and thinking skills while, at the same time, you influence your child's TV choices. Don't be afraid to limit TV watching at other times: otherwise kids won't have sufficient time to devote to other activities. When the weekly TV schedule appears in the newspaper sit down with the kids and plan the week's viewing together. Post the schedule near the TV. Insist that the machine remain off at non-scheduled times.

Video cassette recorders (VCRs) are another helpful tool for controlling TV viewing. With a VCR you can record programs and then watch them at the family's convenience instead of at the scheduled broadcast time. Programs of merit such as "Nova" or *National Geographic* specials can be watched more than once. Kids will no longer need to stay up past their bedtimes to see a holiday special. Even more delightful is the fact that most VCR's allow you to use a fast forward control to skip over the commercials.

Are computers a passing fad like pet rocks? No. They are a most valuable home resource for kids. In fact, many colleges now require computer literacy before allowing their students to graduate. Many state education departments are considering mandating computer literacy as a prerequisite for high school graduation, too. Games, educational software, and word processing functions all will excite kids—and provide direct instruction in specific skills. Three-year-olds can learn the alphabet on a computer. Nine-year-olds can master the multiplication tables. Twelve-year-olds can type reports. If you find the world of computers foreign and frightening to you, it's time to get involved. Many books and magazines are available to give you information about purchasing and using a computer at home.

Other resources in your home should include maps, globes, educational toys and games, pictures, and musical instruments. Emphasize the hobbies and interests of each person in the family. These provide endless opportunities for exploration, sharing, discussion, and growth.

Exploring the Outside World. Expose your children to the larger world of the community. It's catching. Museums, libraries, parks, zoos, historical places of interest, art galleries, concerts, and plays all stimulate kids' interests and intellects. From riding the escalator in a shopping mall to watching ducks in a pond, these activities are sources of family fun as well as opportunities to see, hear, think, and discuss. Don't count on the few meager field trips the kids take with their classes each year to be sufficient exploration of all your community has to offer.

Don't limit your field trips in the community to places and activities. Include visits to meet interesting people. Talking to a policeman or fireman off duty provides an opportunity to learn firsthand how they see themselves and their jobs. One mother I know takes each child, just before his or her eighteenth birthday, to meet the local supervisor of elections for a talk on the importance of voting. Family friends are wonderful adult resources for kids to talk to about the world of work. You can tell their kids about your world while they explain their work to your children.

Such trips into the community are excellent family fun times, too. Your family will grow in feelings of closeness and togetherness as a result of these outings.

Enjoying the World of Nature. Being outside lets children expand and develop their natural curiosity and sense of exploration. Leaves, rocks, creeping critters, streams, clouds, rainbows, all fascinate kids. Outside they can use all their five senses and they can learn to count, classify, and record what they see. Their understanding of math, science, and language can be expanded through outdoor experiences. When the weather turns nice, pack a picnic and head for the nearest woods. Look for and record the first signs of spring. Visit the same spot every other month to observe the changes as the seasons progress. Your local or school library has books filled with dozens of suggestions for outdoor activities that families can enjoy together.

Developing Motor Skills. Encourage activities that develop your kids' bodies. While outside together, emphasize large motor skills such as running, jumping, skipping, hopping, climbing, skating, swimming, riding a bike, and catching and throwing balls. Inside, encourage activities that develop the fine motor skills such as drawing, cutting, pasting, making patterns on pegboards, stringing beads, sewing, and playing with parquetry blocks. DLM, the same company mentioned earlier in reference to language materials, also produces excellent materials for developing fine motor skills. Since educators see a strong connection between motor skills and the development of the perceptual skills necessary for success in reading, make sure your children have ample opportunity to engage in such activities.

Reading Together. Reading aloud is not only for young kids. From Mother Goose to Shakespearian plays, share the world of books and ideas from the time a baby is old enough to sit on your lap and look at the pictures until the time kids finish high school. Much research has been done on the importance of talking to infants even younger than fifteen months; reading aloud is another form of talking. Apparently the foundations of intelligence and academic success are built at this time.

Educators tell us that no activity better motivates kids to want to read well in school. Kids who can read by themselves will still enjoy sitting close to mom or dad and hearing a story that is perhaps just a little more difficult than they could tackle alone. Use the stories as springboards for discussions to foster the development of language, thought, and expression. Jim Trelease, in *The Read-Aloud Handbook,* gives you loads of ideas on reading to kids.

Listening and Playing Music Together. Listen to all types of music together with your kids. Most libraries have excellent record collections from which you can borrow. Sing together—an especially good activity for long car trips. A cheerful round of "Old MacDonald had a Farm" or "You Are My Sunshine" will perk up everyone. The sillier the song, the more fun you'll have. Make some simple instruments. Kids love playing music by humming through combs covered with tissue paper or by plunking out notes and tunes by filling glasses with varying amounts of water. Be sure, however, that you give music lessons only to kids who want to learn. Don't pressure kids to learn an instrument merely because you wish you had learned to play when young. Take lessons yourself if you're the one who wants to learn. A parent learning to play an instrument may even inspire a child to do the same.

There's Still More. Cook together—and learn to measure. Do art projects. Sew. Make projects out of wood or clay. Plant a garden. Just about every activity parents do in the home can involve kids. See their sense of pride and self-confidence grow as they gain useful skills. Make the shared activity a time for conversation and a time to extend your child's knowledge of the world.

Teaching Good Work Habits

Good work habits involve the ability to organize and utilize space and time to their fullest advantage. A few kids—and adults, too—seem to have been born with an uncanny ability to get organized with great ease. The rest of us must acquire our organizational abilities through planned learning experiences and specific actions.

When you teach work habits, remember that you are teaching specific skills, not imposing parental standards to which you expect your kids to adhere. It's not enough just to tell the kids to be neat and efficient. Instead you must create a specific system of organization with them.

R. H. Dave, in his doctoral dissertation written at the University of Chicago, found that kids from homes with clear structures and routines experienced more success in school than kids from homes that lacked basic organization and usually allowed each person to do whatever he or she wanted whenever he or she wanted. Dr. Rudolf Dreikurs, the noted child-behavior expert, expressed very much the same view when he pointed out that rules and routines are to a child as walls are to a house. They provide the basic support upon which everything else is built.

Make sure that there is a well-defined physical structure for your kids: a place to play, a place to eat, a place to study, and a place to sleep. Similarly, you will have to structure a time to play, a time to eat, a time to study, and a time to sleep. Remember, rigidity isn't what you're after, but rather a reassuring consistency and sense of order.

Setting up this kind of organized space and schedule isn't easy for many of us. Parents and kids often have outside activities that interfere with routines at home. If you never learned good organizational skills or work habits yourself, you may find you need to learn many of these skills as you proceed. Don't discourage yourself by setting an impossible goal of one hundred percent organization all of the time with your kids. Think of organization as a process. Every little step you take toward efficient use of time and space in your home is one more little success that will have a positive effect on your kids.

Organizing Space. Let's concentrate on the two areas of the environment most crucial to kids' school success: their rooms and their study area.

Kids' rooms need to be divided into areas that allow for sleeping, dressing, playing, and studying. The last two areas often get jumbled together. It's not easy to start homework if one's desk is covered with a half-built model airplane, scraps of paper from a collage, assorted crayons, books, and so on.

To make any organizational changes stick, it is essential to involve the kids in the task. That way you can teach them the steps involved in organizing an environment. You also will ensure much more cooperation in maintaining the environment when they are a part of the process.

• ANALYZE THE PRESENT USE OF SPACE Begin by looking critically at your kids' rooms. The typical room has many more toys and materials than any child needs, which makes organizing the environment an almost impossible job. The solution to too much stuff is rotation. Decide with your kids what will be used during this month and pack the rest in boxes. Plan a special "un-birthday" next month, when the toys in that box will be unpacked and different ones will be packed away.

• STUDY THE STORAGE SYSTEM How are toys and materials stored in the room? In many rooms, things are just stuffed helter-skelter in toy boxes, dumped in drawers, or crammed on shelves. Instead, set up a specific place to store each item. Encourage your kids to categorize their possessions so that similar items are stored together. Give them loads of containers of all sizes for small collections and such supplies as crayons, scissors, papers, building toys, etc. Coffee cans, shoe boxes, plastic laundry tubs, Tupperware bowls that have lost their lids, all make great storage containers. Once they have each item stored in appropriate containers and/or placed in suitable spots, label each spot. Use a labelmaker or stickers. Draw pictures on stickers for kids who can't read.

Don't despair if it takes many afternoons or an entire weekend to complete this process. The results will be worth it. Imagine always finding something when you want it! Imagine always knowing where to put something when you are finished with it! An organized environment allows a child the freedom to play and learn because whatever he or she needs will be there when it's needed.

• ONCE-A-WEEK CLEANUPS Encourage your kids to maintain an orderly environment by scheduling a regular time each week for clean-up. Post a list of each task you expect your kids to complete, such as:

1. Pick up everything on the floor and return it to its designated storage area.
2. Check each shelf and container to make sure each item corresponds to the label.
3. Return loose items on the desk to their proper storage spot.
4. Dust shelves.
5. Sweep or vacuum floor.

For kids who can't read lists, take pictures of your child performing each of the above tasks and post them next to the words.

If you can't picture such a neat environment or can't imagine that kids can keep it that way, visit a Montessori school in your area. You will see schoolrooms where every item has a specific place—and the children, from two years old up, keep it that way. The secret of success is the effort the adults make with the kids to organize and maintain the environment.

Take particular care in organizing a study area or "home office" for each of your kids. Schooling and homework should be given the same respect and importance as your job. It is, in essence, your kids' employment. Give this office special status and emphasis that will reinforce for the kids the value you put on learning. Be sure it's in an area relatively free from distractions and loud noises. Let them have a sign or nameplate. Put up a bulletin board. Make lists together of everything a home office needs: pencils, pens, erasers, scissors, paper of all kinds, pads, file folders, paper clips, tape, stapler, reference books, maps, globes, etc. Shop together for any items not currently on hand. Once again, you'll need containers and labels so everything can be given a specific place.

Moms and dads carry briefcases; kids need bookbags. Bookbags organize the material that goes back and forth between home and school. Bookbags help eliminate lost notices and assignments, forgotten lunch money, and misplaced library books. Make it a ritual to spend a few minutes with each kid each night looking over the contents of his or her bookbag and talking about his or her studies; this subtly tells your kids the value you place on schoolwork. Have a hook or box by the door where they can place their bookbag before breakfast, so everything is ready to be picked up as they leave.

Organizing Time.   For kids to develop good work habits, they must first have a good sense of time. They must have a good grasp of the amount of time involved in an activity or task and an understanding of the sequence of events. A few kids seem to have an inbred, inherent ability use their time wisely. Most kids, however, need help from their parents in learning to organize their time.

Predictable daily routines for dressing and undressing, eating, sleeping, playing, learning, and cleaning up teach young children that events occur in a time sequence. First we wake up, then we wash, then we dress, then we eat breakfast, etc. It's OK for the steps in your daily routines to be different from those of the family next door—establish routines that meet the preferences and needs of your family. This predictable sequence of events each day gives young kids a sense of control over their lives and allows them to anticipate things that are going to happen. It allows older children to plan their own activities so that the household routine is not interrupted. When you put the daily household routines in sequence, you model for kids a good way of organizing personal activities and commitments, including studying.

Learning to measure time is more difficult than learning to put things in sequence. Most kids today first measure time by the length of an average TV show. A five-year-old who asks "How long will this take?" will understand the parent who responds "The same amount of time 'Sesame Street' takes." Or the same amount as two "Sesame Streets," or half a "Sesame Street." Use any TV show your kids are familiar with as a yardstick.

On certain days make a point of focusing on time. Mention that dinner tonight took thirty minutes, the walk in the park was an hour, clean up was only ten minutes, and so on. Use a kitchen timer for measuring how long activities take and for setting time goals. Give kids an alarm clock of their own. Make sure some of your clocks aren't digital so your kids have a chance to learn to tell time the "old fashioned way" with hour and minute hands. After a while kids will develop an interest in accurately judging time spans.

Talk about setting priorities for the use of time, too. "We have forty-five minutes tonight for a family activity. What shall we choose to do that takes that long?" To use time well you must make choices, see what fits, plan for all contingencies. When families plan activities together, kids gain experience in making choices and setting priorities.

Schedules and calendars can teach kids to use time wisely, too. By creating their own activity schedules, kids learn more than they do from relying on parents to remind them.

Young children need a very simple daily schedule that lists chores to be done, homework assignments, and any other commitments, such as plans to play with a friend or a trip to the dentist. In the beginning you'll need to plan this schedule with each kid. You can do this at any convenient time: before he goes to bed at night, at the breakfast table, or when the kids come home from school. As they become familiar with scheduling, you will not need to be involved with their schedules on a daily basis. Be around to encourage them and to give support and suggestions when necessary, but give your kids the main responsibility for creating their own schedule. Post each child's schedule in a prominent place: on the refrigerator door, on a bulletin board, or in the kids' home office. Where you put it doesn't matter as long as the place is consistent each day.

By the time kids are in second or third grade, weekly calendars showing schedules for each day are advisable. These calendars help kids plan across longer periods of time.

In the upper elementary grades and above, pocket calendars are useful for keeping track of even longer periods of time and can be carried around for handy planning.

Guiding Your Child's Efforts

It's not enough just to stimulate your child's intellect and teach good organizational skills. All through the school years you will have to encourage your child's progress and guide his efforts toward success by dealing with homework and grades.

Homework is an issue that can cause great trouble between parents, kids, and teachers. If kids don't turn in their assignments neatly, correctly, and on time, teachers often call or send notes home asking the parents to be sure their kids do their homework. Yet when parents try to force their kids to do the work, battles of major proportions frequently erupt. The kids get mad at the parents. The parents get mad at the teachers. Kids learn to play their parents against their teachers to get the adults fighting, thereby taking the focus off themselves. What's needed are clearcut guidelines outlining the responsibilities of parents, teachers, and kids for completing homework assignments.

Teachers assign homework to children. The responsibility to complete this work belongs to the kids. The task of establishing incentives for finishing homework and consequences for not completing homework belongs to the teachers.

You can, however, take steps that encourage your kids to complete their homework. In addition to organizing time and space efficiently, you can plan the daily household routine to include a specific time for kids to be in their home offices studying and completing homework. Benjamin Bloom, in his book *All Our Children Learning,* cites the positive effect on kids' school achievement when study time is given priority in the home.

Notice that there's a difference between scheduling a study time in the home and forcing kids to do a specific assignment. You don't want to enter into power struggles over homework. Instead, you want to communicate the value you place on learning by making time for it a priority in the daily schedule.

Make this study time consistent Monday through Thursday. On days when no homework has been given or assignments are finished before the study time is over, kids can read and do other quiet study activities in their special home office. Put the telephone off limits during study time. Keep a very positive attitude toward this study time. It's really a time of opportunity, a time of exploration, a time to reinforce new learnings. If you consider it a drudgery, so will the kids. In fact, if you can find the time in your own busy schedule, plan a quiet time of your own when you sit and read and model for your children just how valuable you think learning really is.

When should this study time take place? Again, that's a matter of individual preferences. In some homes it's best to study right after school. In others a break from schoolwork is needed and kids study best after supper. This is a decision that is best made by kids and parents together—to impose your will is to invite defiance and disobedience. It's also OK to allow different kids in the same family to schedule different times for studying. Again, individual differences can be accepted as long as each child has a specific time set aside.

The younger the child, the more you need to be involved in scheduling this study time and seeing that he or she adheres to it. As kids get older, if homework is consistently done and grades are acceptable, you can bow out and only become involved if your child asks you to or if problems develop. If problems do develop and kids are not working well during this time, use what's known as Grandma's Law—first we work, then we play. Schedule study time before a fun activity, such as playing with friends or watching TV. Then there is a built-in incentive to finish the work and go on to something else.

You can also encourage kids to complete homework by being available for help when needed. Remember, helping your kids does not involve completing assignments for them. You want to reinforce their school learnings, not do it for them. If you find your child asking for excessive help, or if he or she has difficulty completing tasks more often than once a week, make an appointment to talk to the teacher.

Extra help with academic skills needs to come from a teacher or a tutor rather than from a parent. Even parents who are willing to help teach frequently get into difficulty because it's so hard to be objective about their own child's learning. When our kid doesn't catch on immediately, we often become frustrated and upset. Our own self worth seems threatened because we often see our kids as extensions of ourselves. The child, sensing our feelings, also becomes upset. He or she feels insecure about his or her own abilities. Tears quickly follow, unkind words are said, the evening is ruined and the homework still is incomplete. Back off if homework is turning into unhappy hassles and leave the teaching to the teacher.

Schoolwork Displays Encourage your kids to be proud of their schoolwork by displaying their papers and art work. If you need extra space to hang things, you can make large, inexpensive bulletin boards by covering 4' × 8' sheets of pressed board with burlap. Some families cover an entire wall with these bulletin boards. Your kids will appreciate seeing their schoolwork on display. You can even have scheduled showings for each child and invite neighbors and relatives to the "opening."

At the end of the study time, you can check over your kids' work. Do this frequently for young children who are just learning to complete assignments at home. Use this time to talk about the work and answer any questions that your kids might have. When the routine is well established, if there are few errors and no problems, you may not need to do this every day unless you and the kids enjoy the routine and wish it to continue. The general rule is that the younger the child, or the more difficulties he experiences, the more guidance and supervision you must give.

Grades, like homework, belong to the child. Your response to them should be to focus on the child's feelings and reactions, not on your own. You want your kids to be motivated to do well to please themselves, to meet their own goals, to prepare themselves for future achievements and successes.

When they receive good grades, ask them how they feel and what specific things they did to achieve so much success, thus encouraging them to continue in the same manner. When they receive poor grades, let them ventilate all their feelings. You may hear excuses, complaints, and blame placed elsewhere. Just listen, don't contradict or attempt to prove your child mistaken. Later, when the feelings have calmed down, talk to your child about his or her plans for the coming marking period. What can he or she do to improve his or her grades? Are there some things that could be done differently in school? At home? Ask your child specifically if there's anything he or she would like you to do to help.

Homework Hotline Students in Hillsborough County, Florida, experiencing difficulties completing their assignments can pick up the phone and dial a teacher for homework help anytime between 3 PM and 8 PM each weekday. It's a wonderful way to keep the homework responsibility where it belongs—between kids and teachers. The homework hotline leaves parents free to provide support and encouragement without getting involved in the direct teaching of skills.

It's important not to let your child manipulate you with grades or use them as a weapon. If you demonstrate that good grades please you and poor grades upset you, your child may use school work as a way to win your approval or provoke you instead of concentrating on learning for its own sake. Many kids fail a course or two just to get back at parents for something that angers them. Demonstrate interest and stay involved in your kids' schooling, but minimize the importance of grades per se, and allow the child to experience the pleasure of good grades and the pain of poor grades. In this way you lay the groundwork for helping your child choose to perform more satisfactorily in the future.

When you approach your child's education as an ongoing process that he or she will have to take responsibility for as time passes, efforts to stimulate, organize, and guide kids make more sense than just seeing that homework gets done. These tasks are much bigger and much more important in developing learning skills because they'll be used throughout life. But the results will show up right away, too. When parents are providing so much support at home, teachers recognize it and have the time and incentive for dealing productively with homework at school.

3

•••••••••••••••••••••••••••••••

How to Motivate
Your Kids to the
Head of the Class

"I can't do my math homework, Mom, I just don't know how."
"I can't read this story, Dad, the words are too big." "Will
somebody help me with my chores? I can't set up the vacuum
and it's my turn to do the floors." There goes Teddy again,
with his same old refrain—"I can't, I can't, I can't." His
teachers says it's the same story in school—he refuses to do
anything by himself because he says he "can't." He will work
only when the teacher is standing right beside him. "Is this a
stage all eight-year-olds go through," you wonder, "or is there
a way to motivate Teddy to say 'I can' instead of 'I can't'?"

Another poor report card for Janet! No wonder—she
spends too much time with her stamp collection and other
hobbies when she should be reading and studying. You keep

telling her she'll never succeed in school if she doesn't try harder, and warning her that she'll be just like her cousin Brenda, a dropout at sixteen. Even showing her how much better her younger sister Karen is doing at school doesn't seem to make Janet work harder. Her teacher says Janet does poorly in school because she's "not motivated." What can you do to make her want to work harder in school and study more at home?

Nick gets lots of attention from everyone. He's always doing something he's not supposed to do: fighting with his brother and sister, making a mess, or dawdling when it's time to eat or get dressed and ready for school. No amount of yelling, criticism or punishment seems to change his behavior. You'd much prefer to give him positive attention in place of all the negative attention he now receives, but how on earth do you motivate a child to do something right for a change?

A motivated person, according to the *Oxford American Dictionary,* is one who has a definite and positive desire to do things. Despite all the negative press our schools have been getting lately, kids who have a definite and positive desire to learn can and usually do succeed in school. This chapter details how you can motivate your children by adopting an effective parenting style, establishing an encouraging family atmosphere, focusing on "I Can's" instead of "IQs," and removing the payoffs for poor school performance.

Motivating your child is a process, not a one-shot deal. The process starts in infancy and continues all through the school years. You won't see immediate results, nor will progress be continuous. The more time and effort you put into motivating your children, the less time you will have to spend solving academic and behavior problems in school.

Developing Effective Parenting Techniques

Over the last few years, the Gallup Poll of public attitudes consistently ranks discipline as one of the major problems of American education. Parents blame teachers, saying they should learn how to control kids in their classes. Teachers blame parents, saying kids who aren't disciplined effectively at home can't be expected to behave at school. We have already noted that placing blame solves nothing. Instead let's admit that discipline is a tough task for both parents and teachers. What you can do to motivate your children to behave in school is to adopt an effective parenting style that will allow you to discipline your kids effectively.

The chart that follows describes three parenting styles. Study it carefully and analyze your own behavior to see which style fits.*

You will be able to discipline your kids most effectively if you adopt the democratic style of parenting. This style teaches kids self-control and self-discipline. They learn to follow established rules and routines not because someone will punish them if they don't, but because they experience the positive rewards of cooperation when they do. This style promotes good communication and mutual respect within the family by involving kids in decisions that affect them.

Although many of us grew up successfully with parents who used the autocratic style of parenting, this style doesn't work well today. We see few places left in society where any group of people unquestioningly accepts the authority of another group. The autocratic style of parenting invites non-cooperation and rebellion from our kids. They may behave well in our presence out of fear of punishment, but they do not develop internal control that will serve them out of the home.

---

*L. Albert and E. Einstein, "Stepfamily Living: Dealing with Discipline" (Tampa, FL: privately published, 1983).

DISCIPLINE STYLES

	AUTHORITARIAN	DEMOCRATIC	PERMISSIVE
Role of the parent	boss	leader; guide	servant; bystander
Characteristics of the parent	overbearing dictatorial inflexible strict repressive uncompromising tyrannical dominating	approachable respected reasonable flexible encouraging	fearful inconsistent indecisive yielding passive weak
Role of the child	to obey	to think to contribute to cooperate	to control others to follow own wants and instincts
Who's got the power?	the parent	shared between parent and child	the child
Home atmosphere	tense rigid militaristic oppressive	relaxed orderly consistent	chaotic uncontrolled wild
Discipline tools	yelling commanding ordering rewarding punishing	incentives consequences assertion messages negotiation conflict resolution	pleading wishing waiting giving up and doing nothing yielding

	bribing threatening	family councils automatic rules and routines established requesting limited chores	
Effect on the child	obeys out of fear of punishment; subverts and manipulates underhandedly; often out of control when parents aren't present; develops little self control; retaliates; strikes out at times	develops self-discipline; is able to focus on the needs of the group	becomes self-centered and demanding; fails to develop consideration of others or of needs of the group; develops little self-control
Quality of parent/child relationship	fear; distance; coldness; resentment; rigidity	close; open; sharing; respectful; communicative	distant; resentful; child may feel unloved, uncared for; manipulative
Historical background	most of us raised this way	few prepared to discipline in this style; few raised this way; potentially can be taught to all parents	some of us raised this way; often used when parents didn't want to be autocratic and thought this the only alternative; some parents swing like a pendulum between this and authoritarian style

In fact, fear of punishment often teaches kids not to change their behavior but to become more sneaky in order to avoid being caught next time they repeat the misbehavior. In this style of parenting, kids don't learn to think for themselves and to consider beforehand the consequences of their actions.

The permissive style is frequently used by parents who are discouraged about finding skills and techniques that they can successfully use to discipline their kids. Very often these parents have rejected the autocratic style on philosophical grounds, but haven't found an effective replacement for it. The lack of order, disrespect for others, and self-centeredness this style fosters will not prepare kids to succeed in a classroom with twenty or thirty other children.

Parental Mistakes Everyone makes mistakes. Parents are no exception. Occasionally every parent does or says something to his child that he or she later regrets. Yet some parents feel that they must never admit their mistakes by apologizing to their children. These parents believe that somehow their authority will be undermined if their kids see that they can be "wrong." The opposite is true. By admitting mistakes and apologizing to their kids, parents model an important attitude: it's OK not to be perfect, it's OK to make and admit mistakes. A child will respect you more when you show respect for him by apologizing.

It is possible to raise kids today with a high degree of self-discipline, a strong sense of independence, a willingness to cooperate, and feelings of self-confidence. You can do this by learning the discipline tools listed on pages 34–35 under the "Democratic Style." You needn't fear losing control in the family when you use the democratic parenting tools. Involving kids in making decisions doesn't mean you must always accept their ideas and suggestions. It does mean, however, that kids will be part of the process of arriving at family decisions. The key word is *process.*

The subject of effective discipline is covered in great detail in the companion volume to this book, *Linda Albert's Advice for Coping with Kids.* In addition, you may find joining a parent study group an enjoyable way to improve your skills. See Appendix 1 for resource information on such programs.

Establishing an Encouraging Family Atmosphere

When you provide each child with the necessary four A's: attention, appreciation, affection, and acceptance, you encourage your children to be successful in school. These four A's fulfill each child's need to feel loved and significant within the family.

Attention will make each of your kids feel that he or she belongs to the family in a special way. Avoid the common mistake of giving more attention to kids when they misbehave than when they behave appropriately. Think how much easier it often is for a child to get your attention for poor grades or a fight in school than for not failing, not fighting. You want to provide quality attention on a regular basis and make it clear that you are more impressed by successes than failures.

Each of your children needs a few minutes of time alone with you each day. The length of time you spend isn't as important as how the time is spent. Let your child bring up topics and share what is on his mind. Learn to really listen to your kids. Don't use this time for talking about misbehavior or giving advice. Once or twice a week plan longer periods during which you invite your child to join you in an activity.

Plan special occasions to celebrate events and successes—no matter how great or small—in each kid's life. Learning to read a new book, painting an original picture, mastering a new tune on the piano, making a new friend, getting a good mark on a test or report card, are all good occasions for special attention. Children love the fun and fuss of celebrations and treasure memories of them long afterward. You can keep the memories alive in scrapbooks with photographs and stories about the events. The celebrations need not be elaborate. They could be as simple as a special toast at dinner time or a handshake or pat on the back from each member of the family. Use your imagination.

Express your appreciation often. A child's self-esteem thrives in an atmosphere where the positive comments greatly outweigh the negative. Discard any old fashioned notions you might have about too much praise swelling a child's head! The opposite is true—too little praise shrinks self-confidence and saps motivation to succeed.

Don't wait too long before expressing appreciation, or set standards so high that kids have little chance of reaching them. Notice the little steps kids accomplish as they work toward a larger goal. Comment positively on efforts and good intentions, and on the things kids do to contribute to the whole family's well being. Let them repeat their successes frequently; each time they do you have another chance to express appreciation.

Lots of affection, both verbal and physical, is also important for kids. Don't make affection contingent upon good behavior or attach any strings to it. It's OK to let kids know that you dislike their misbehavior, but at the same time be sure they understand that you still love them. The ability to separate the behavior from the person, the deed from the doer, is key to being able to maintain positive feelings about your child while taking appropriate action to correct misbehaviors.

Let your kids know you accept them as they are—their good points and their bad, their strengths and their weaknesses, their successes and their failures. As one eight-year-old pleaded, "Be nice to me, Mom, God isn't finished with me yet."

Acceptance means allowing your kids to be different from

you. They may choose different clothes, fancy different foods, like different music, enjoy different subjects, prefer different activities. Being different isn't necessarily good or bad—it's just different. Avoid pressuring your kids to live up to your image. Don't compare them to siblings, relatives, or neighbors. The more freedom you give them to be themselves, the more cooperative, respectful, and successful they'll be at home and at school.

Repeat Compliments Part of building your child's self-esteem is giving compliments. Some children apparently experience difficulty hearing and acknowledging compliments. Such kids shrug their shoulders and walk away as if your positive words have little value. These children need to hear the compliments repeated over and over until the message is received and recorded internally. Ignore the old adage that too many compliments will make a child conceited or self-centered. Repeat compliments often. It's the way to make sure your child has a strong self-image. Every child deserves one.

What you ask for is usually what you get, even when raising kids. Dwell on their failures and predict terrible futures, and watch your kids live up to these images. Expect success and predict wonderful futures, and see how positively your kids are motivated. Since your words and images define your kids' world today and in the future, be sure you paint a happy, successful picture.

Focusing on "I Can" Instead of on "IQ" or "I Can't"

Research tells us that kids who succeed in school generally possess a high level of self-esteem. Your child will develop such self-esteem more from a strong belief in, and utilization of, his abilities rather than from his IQ score. You can easily raise your children's "I Can" quotient. The secret is to stop doing things for your kids that they can do for themselves and to stop noticing and focusing on their mistakes.

Most of us do too much for our kids. We wash their clothes when they are perfectly capable of running a washer and dryer by themselves. We remind them to do homework and to take lunch money when they have perfectly good memories. We make their beds, spoon food onto their plates, pick up the towels they drop on the bathroom floor, and tell them which shirt to wear. Most kids rarely complain about the extra services they receive—they are content to take it easy and let us shoulder their responsibilities. In fact they sometimes even complain when we stop doing all this for them.

Why might parents do too much for their kids? It makes some parents feel needed, important, and useful. They feel it is a parents' job to perform all these functions. Others do too much because in the short run it's easier and quicker to do things yourself than to teach your kids to do them. Other parents do too much because they feel guilty about something—maybe a separation or divorce, or a disability or handicap with which a child must cope. Some parents are perfectionists. Their kids can rarely do things in a way that meets their unrealistic standards. These parents often see their kids' less than perfect abilities as proof of their own parental inadequacy. Doing things for their kids spares them the need to deal with their feelings of inadequacy.

The sad effect of doing too much for our kids, whatever our motivation or intention, is that we build up the kids' "I can't" quotient and thus lower their self-esteem. "I can'ts" lead to feelings of inadequacy and fears of failure. Kids with such feelings often stop trying to succeed. It's not that they aren't motivated and wouldn't like to succeed; rather it's that they don't feel they have a chance to do well, so they refuse to make any effort.

In addition to seldom doing things for your kids that they can do for themselves, give attention and appreciation for every "I can" your kid achieves. Take pictures of the "I can's", make lists of them, tell Grandma and the neighbors all about them. Allow them to be repeated over and over again. Watch how the "I cans" at home carry over into "I cans" at school.

Minimizing mistakes will also increase your children's "I can" level. The essential learning process is being shown something new, trying it, making a mistake, analyzing what went wrong, and trying again. Ideally the process is repeated until success is achieved. When parents focus on mistakes, the learning process breaks down. The sense of embarrassment and failure kids experience stops them from analyzing what went wrong and trying again. Give up any ideas you have that parents are supposed to point out mistakes for everyone to see as a way to motivate their kids to do better next time. In reality focusing on mistakes usually lowers kids' self-esteem and discourages future efforts. Instead focus on their successes and on each bit of improvement they make.

Help your children accept mistakes. Tell them that mistakes are OK, that making mistakes is part of learning. In a natural, matter-of-fact manner, talk about your own mistakes and describe how you plan from them. Encourage everyone in the family to talk openly about their mistakes. When kids can talk about mistakes openly, without fear of being criticized or embarrassed, their fear and failures diminish and their motivation to try again until they succeed increases.

Redirecting Kids' Mistaken Purposes for Misbehavior

Earlier in this chapter we defined a motivated person as one who has a positive desire to do things. We want our kids to have a positive desire to learn, and have been exploring ways we can increase this motivation. Now we need to look at the payoffs some kids get for not learning and for misbehaving in school. By taking action to prevent these payoffs, we can redirect our kids' behavior for success instead of failure.

One payoff kids get for doing poorly in school is lots of extra attention. Stop and think, for a minute, of all the attention a poor reader gets. His parents are called to school for a conference, special testing is given, a tutor or aide may be assigned for extra reading practice, often books or trinkets are offered as a reward for improvement. I'm not suggesting that we ignore poor readers, simply that we shift our emphasis. The amount of attention we give to success and positive behavior in school must be more than the amount of attention we give to misbehavior. The chapters that follow outline appropriate steps you can take to remediate problems in school. Remember, however, to always give more attention to what is right than to what is wrong.

Keep in Touch   The psychological importance of touching your child doesn't diminish with age. Kisses, hugs, pats, hand squeezes, and an arm around the waist all encourage warm, close feelings and strengthen the bond between you. Little kids love rub-downs and massages. Big kids do, too, but often are too embarrassed to admit it. Continue touching to keep close to your kids.

Another payoff kids may get for doing poorly in school is the chance to play boss, to show that nobody can make them do anything they don't want to do. Some kids play boss very actively—they clearly state their intention of ignoring you. Others are more passive and subtle—they agree with you, often say they will do what you want, and then proceed to do exactly what they wanted to do in the first place.

When dealing with kids who like to play boss, you will have to learn to sidestep the power struggles. Fighting with them, or using your power to overcome them, usually leads to more fights, more defiance, and, often, outright rebellion. Most punishments backfire. Parental pressure has little effect. What does work is involving the kids in analyzing the problems at school and in devising the steps to be taken to solve these problems. Consequences can be established for their misbehaviors as long as the kids are involved in setting the consequences. By involving the kids in the solution, you give them legitimate power that wins their cooperation and motivates them to succeed.

Yet another payoff is revenge. Kids can use school failure to get even with parents by hurting and disappointing them. Why should a child want to get even with a parent? Sometimes it's in response to excessive pressure to perform, sometimes it's because they feel they have been unfavorably compared to a sibling, other times it's because they feel unfairly treated. There are endless possibilities.

To redirect revenge behavior, we have to sidestep our feelings of hurt and disappointment. Showing these feelings to your children will not motivate them to change their behavior; rather it will show them just how effective their behavior is. Deal with the behaviors as you would with power struggles— involve your children in setting up consequences and solutions. Focus heavily on any areas of success. Increase the amounts of attention, appreciation, affection and acceptance that you give your children.

Poor school performance is only one way kids get extra attention, engage parents in power struggles, or seek revenge. Bedtime, mealtime, getting dressed, relationships with siblings—any situation at home is a potential conflict area. When you deal successfully with your kids' misbehaviors in these areas, you can expect a positive carry-over to school situations involving similar dynamics. Remove the payoffs for misbehaviors in all areas of your children's lives and watch their motivation to learn improve dramatically.

4

....

How to Establish an Effective Home-School Partnership

How many times have you grumbled to a neighbor, "My kid would be having a good year in school if only he had a better teacher. A teacher who cared more. Who tried harder. Who seemed to like kids more. Who had better training. Who knew how to make the kids behave."

How many times have you listened to your kids complain about school and commiserated with them about how awful schools and teachers are?

How many times have you skipped an open house, a PTA function, or a conference because you felt that since nothing could change "the system," you might as well not waste your time?

In order to cope successfully with your child's education, begin to see yourself as part of a team. The central members of that team will be you, your child, and the teacher. By establishing a cooperative relationship with the teacher you are taking the first essential step in building a team that can function smoothly and serve the best interests of your child. Unless such a cooperative effort exists, your child will have less than optimum opportunities for learning.

It's important that both parents consider themselves part of the team. Schools are no longer places just for Moms. Just Dad's presence will communicate both to your kids and their teachers his belief in the value of education. Dad's insights, observations and suggestions will be helpful when there are problems to be solved.

Don't Wait   You don't need a specific reason to drop in to say "hello" to your children's teachers. There doesn't have to be a problem to be solved, nor does it have to be time for a formal conference. In fact, you needn't talk about the kids at all! "Hi, I'm glad to see you today" is sufficient. You might take a couple of minutes to chat about some topic or activity of interest to the teacher or to express your appreciation of the teacher's efforts. The purpose of these brief meetings is to cement your relationship with the teachers and to keep the lines of communication open.

Do not expect the teacher to be responsible for establishing contact and managing the team. A teacher who teaches all subjects to the same kids in a self-contained classroom may have twenty-five or thirty kids in his or her classroom. That means the teacher is part of twenty-five or thirty different teams! In schools where kids switch classes for different subjects, teachers can be a part of fifty, one hundred, even one hundred and fifty different parent-teacher teams! Depending upon the number of children you have in school, you are part of either one or a very few parent-teacher-child teams. You, therefore, are in the better position to take the initiative for building a strong team.

A common goal unites this parent-teacher-child team: the growth and success of your child in school. Why, then, does the team break down so frequently? Why do parents and teachers seem to pull against each other instead of supporting each other?

When a child experiences difficulties in school, it's tempting (and very human) for parents to point their fingers at the teachers and blame them for the problem. Teachers do the same thing—they say that if the parents would do more at home their kids would experience fewer difficulties. Remember the snake in the story in Chapter 1. Mutual blame keeps anyone from taking responsibility for solving the problem at hand. As long as we worry about who "caused" the problem we don't look for solutions. Such blaming makes people defensive, too, and unwilling to help each other.

Another common problem is that we often tend to engage in a lot of catastrophic thinking. We see too many problems as unmanageable and unsolvable, especially when we can't find instant solutions to them. Sometimes we forget that building something means laying one brick at a time. As a result we fail to take appropriate action to improve the situation.

No question about it—your kids will greatly benefit from a supportive home-school relationship. Problems that arise can be solved before they become major. Teachers will tend to notice and pay a little more attention to your kids when they are on good terms with you. Become involved with the school and you will impress upon your kids the value of a good education. Communicate frequently and informally with your kids' teachers and your kids cannot play one adult against the other. Your kids will be forced to take responsibility for their own behavior and learning.

Thus a supportive parent-teacher relationship benefits everyone involved. Building this relationship will take time. The rest of this chapter will outline the steps you need to take.

Fill Up on Facts

Q. Lately there has been so much criticism and negative information about schools in the news that I want to learn more about the particular schools my children attend. How do you suggest I go about this?

A. Educational researchers at Cornell University recommend the seven methods listed below for getting to know your child's school better:
- make an appointment to visit
- drop in to look around and talk with people
- call or write to teachers or principals
- talk with other parents and children about their experiences
- read school-board minutes in the newspaper
- read the school newsletter
- attend school functions, especially open houses and PTA meetings

The more of these methods you use, the better. Getting a complete, balanced picture requires more than one or two of these steps.

Call the school secretary to see if drop-in visits are allowed. If not, make an advance appointment. Don't generalize too much from one visit. Think of someone dropping in to your home or office unannounced—is what they would see at the moment typical of your entire day? Your entire week? Use this visit to gather impressions that you must balance with the information you get from the other sources.

Be just as careful with information gathered from other parents and children. Some people magnify negative experiences out of proportion. Ask questions that will give a rounded view. For example, when talking with another parent ask what they did and didn't like about a specific teacher and what they saw as both the strengths and weaknesses of the classroom program.

Read school newsletters for information on procedures and policies. Often you'll find general curriculum information as well as introductions to new teachers in the building. Attend "Back to School Nights" most schools hold for parents early in the year. This is the time teachers tell what they will be teaching the children, show parents the material to be used, describe their teaching methods and explain how they manage the class and deal with discipline.

Read accounts of the school board meetings for information on district-wide policies, procedures for hiring and evaluating teachers, enrollment figures and plans, if any, to deal with projected declining enrollment. Better yet, attend the meetings yourself.

General knowledge of the educational issues in your community plus information on what's happening in your child's particular school provides a strong foundation for getting involved in your child's education.

Hellos Help

Q. I want to establish a good relationship with each of my children's teachers this year. The school doesn't schedule conferences and open-houses until at least October. Do I need to wait until then or are there some things I can do earlier in the school term to make contact?

A. Start now. While open houses and conferences are excellent ways to learn more about your children's program and performance in school, you can informally open the lines of communication earlier in the year.

Send a brief "hello" note to each teacher. Express your hopes that the year will be successful for your child and your willingness to do what you can to ensure that success by providing home support. Invite the teacher to send you any information or suggestions that might be helpful now or anytime during the school year. Include a positive comment about something your child has already experienced during the first few days or something you have heard about this teacher from other parents. If you can, volunteer to help when needed. Can you help supervise field trips? Talk with the kids about your work or share a hobby? Bake for parties? This "hello" note begins the friendship and states your intention to be involved and to establish a cooperative parent–teacher relationship.

Issue Invitations Get to know teachers by inviting them to out-of-school functions involving groups of parents. You might organize an evening coffee hour with some other parents and invite one teacher as the guest of honor. You can take turns each month, until each parent has had a turn hosting a coffee hour with a different teacher. Perhaps your church or synagogue has a social hour after the service on Saturday or Sunday where a teacher could mingle informally with parents. Consider inviting teachers to meetings of any organization to which you belong. The better you know the teachers, particularly the non-classroom specialists, the more you will be able to utilize their services for your kids.

Follow this note with a brief informal visit. Perhaps when you need to pick up your child for a medical appointment during the day you can catch the teacher enjoying a break. Or you can arrange to stop in for a minute before or after school. Don't try to have a lengthy discussion about your child at this time. All you want to do is establish a personal relationship with the teacher and thus help communication between home and school flow more easily.

Send frequent notes of appreciation to the teacher; these notes let him know how much you value his efforts. Let him know when you've noticed a new skill your child has acquired. Express your delight when your child comes home happy and excited by some experience he or she has had that day. Send the notes with the kids. They'll benefit too by knowing that you care enough about what's happening in their classroom to write.

Care About Conferences

Q. Because I'm working full-time, attending a parent-teacher conference isn't easy for me—getting extra time off from my job entails a real hassle. How valuable are these conferences? What will I learn that isn't on my kids' report cards?

A. Report cards represent one-way information from the teacher to the parent evaluating their kids' progress. Conferences represent two-way information sharing between teachers and parents that enables everyone to deal more effectively with the child. Expect the following benefits from parent-teacher conferences:

• Strengthening of the cooperative relationship between the parents and teacher

• Exchange of information that will help the teacher work more effectively with the child in school and the parents cope more effectively at home

• Clarification of educational and behavioral expectations

• Discussion of any misunderstandings between home and school. Any tales that the child carries from home to school or vice-versa can be investigated

• Exploration of options and resources to solve problems at school or at home

• Suggestion of home educational experiences that the teacher feels would benefit your child, especially if remediation or enrichment is necessary

Most teachers are flexible and willing to accommodate parents who cannot come to school between 9 AM and 3 PM. Perhaps you can schedule the conference before or after work or in the evening. However you arrange it, know that it will be time well-spent for the sake of your child's success in school.

How to Prepare for a Conference

Q. I'm surprised by how many questions teachers have asked me about my child during conferences. If I knew in advance what kind of information they wanted I probably could give more complete answers. What can I do to prepare for the next conference?

A. Since conferences are a two-way exchange of information between teachers and parents, be prepared to give the teacher information about your child's behavior, activities, and attitudes at home. Here are some of the areas teachers frequently wish to discuss:

● Health and medical needs: Are there any problems that might interfere with your child's activities or performance? Any medication that should be given at school? Be sure that your child has had a medical check-up within the last year and that all immunizations are up-to-date.

● Interests, hobbies, and outside activities: How does your child spend his spare time? Is he able to amuse himself? Does he choose individual or group activities? Does he seem very competitive? Does he spend time at home reading? What kind of books? How much time does he spend watching TV?

● Relationships with other children: How well does your child get along with brothers and sisters? Neighborhood children? Does he seem to make friends easily? Have a lot of friends? Is your child a loner? Does he solve his own problems with other kids or does he run to you to ask for help?

• Relationships with parents: How well does your child listen to you? Does he insist on having his own way frequently? Any temper tantrums? Does he do chores and cooperate within the family unit? Any particular problem areas, such as mealtime or bedtime?

• Independence level: Does your child take care of his own personal hygiene needs? His clothes? His room? Can he get ready for school on time without a lot of nagging and reminding?

• Attitude towards school: What sort of attitude does your child express to you about his teachers, his classmates, and his studies?

• Special circumstances: Is anything happening within the family that would affect the child in school? A serious illness? An impending separation or divorce? If the child does not live with both parents, what is the visiting schedule? Which parent should be called and under which circumstances?

In addition to preparing answers to questions a teacher might ask, make a list of any problems and concerns you want to bring up. It's a good idea to keep a file on each of your children. Put all report cards and samples of the child's work in this cumulative file. Review the file before the conference. Do you notice any changes this year from the performance of previous years? If so, write these down, clip them to the papers from the file that seem relevant, and bring them to the conference. Because you have more direct knowledge of your child's past performance, you are in a position to spot changes and incipient problems before a teacher does.

Reread your school's handbook at this time. In it you should find information about the school's curriculum, philosophy, goals, teaching methods, promotion requirements, and policies concerning attendance, discipline, homework, and grading. List any questions you have concerning how your child's teacher implements these policies. If your school has no handbook you may be able to get this information from an open house, the PTA, or the principal. Gather as much of this information as possible from sources other than your child's teacher so that the conference can focus on your child rather than on general policies.

As you can see, a parent needs to prepare for a conference almost as much as a teacher does.

Parent Centers Every school has a "teachers' room" where teachers can lounge informally, away from students. Some also have a parents' room or center. Parents are welcome to drop in at any time during the day to relax, have a cup of coffee, browse through the parent library shelf, and chat with other parents. Administrators and teachers often drop in to say hello when they have a spare minute. Parent centers are important because they give parents a place of their own in the school. Declining enrollment leaves many schools with spare classrooms that could be turned into such centers with a little effort and imagination. Start one today.

Guidelines for a Successful Conference

Q. Through the years I've attended many parent-teacher conferences. Some have been successful, others seem to go nowhere and accomplish little. Can you tell me why this is, and what I can do about it?

A. The success of parent-teacher conferences depends largely on the attitudes and behaviors of both the parents and the teacher. You have no control over what the teacher does. But if you are careful to follow these guidelines the chances for a successful conference will increase more than fifty percent because what you do will influence the teacher to do the same.

Come fully prepared with observations about the child's home behavior and questions about his or her school development. Let the teacher know ahead of time if you wish to focus on one particular aspect of your child's development so that he or she, too, can be prepared.

Allow enough time for the conference so you do not feel pressure to get back to the office or home to make dinner. Feel free to ask the teacher ahead of time how long he or she expects the conference to last. Then add extra time for unpredictable situations. Sometimes conferences run longer than the teacher anticipates because parents have a lot of questions. Also the teacher may be behind schedule if other conferences preceed yours.

Don't bring young children who will distract you from the conversation—hire a babysitter or leave them with a neighbor instead. It's worth the expense and inconvenience to be able to give the conference your full attention.

Describe your child as honestly as you can to the teacher. Set out his strengths and weaknesses as you see them. Ask the teacher to be as honest with you.

Talk about your child's weaknesses and difficulties in school without defensiveness. To do this separate your own feelings of self-worth from the successes and failures of your kids. Don't be embarrassed by your children's school problems—these do not necessarily reflect your abilities as a parent. No child grows up without some problems, no matter how loving and skillful his parents. Part of the job of a parent is to help identify and solve these problems. Hiding the problems because of parental embarrassment only makes the situation worse.

Avoid blaming and attacking the teacher for any difficulties your child may be experiencing. Such behaviors will make the teacher anxious and defensive. In response, he will often attempt to shift the blame to you and suggest that problems at home are causing the problems in school. Stay away from focusing on whose fault the problem is. Instead, focus on how to solve the problem.

View problems as challenges that need solutions. Avoid being pessimistic and seeing the problems as unmanageable or catastrophic. Solving problems is a process—don't expect quick answers and instant results. Be content with identifying the problems and devising plans to work on them. After the conference, encourage yourself by taking note of every bit of improvement as it occurs.

Be prepared for a balance of talking and listening during the conference. Always ask for clarification if the teacher uses terms you don't understand. Teachers often forget that some of their educational jargon is foreign to parents and rarely resent being asked for definitions. You won't appear dumb by asking—rather, you'll appear interested and alert.

Be generous in expressing your appreciation to the teacher. For his time. For his interest. For his openness, honesty, and courtesy in dealing with you. For any special attention he has given your child. Appreciation makes a teacher feel valued and encourages his willingness to continue helping your child.

Happygrams Teachers often send home Happygrams, short notes to parents describing specific successes their child experienced in school that day. Reverse the process. Send Happygrams to teachers expressing your appreciation when you notice that your child has acquired a new skill or when he or she shows excitement about something that's happened in school. Teachers deserve the good feelings that come when they know that parents notice their efforts.

Should you get upset and say something to the teacher that you later regret having said, it's not the end of the world. The chances are you haven't destroyed the teacher's willingness to cooperate with you or your child forever. Simply send a note of apology and let the matter drop.

Conference Content

Q. What information should I expect to get from the teacher at a school conference? Often so much is talked about that by the time I get home and try to explain what was said to my spouse I can't remember all the details. Will the teacher get upset if I take notes?

A. Avoid this problem completely by taking your spouse with you to the conference. However, you still may want a record of what the teacher had to say. Bring a checklist of the topics to be covered. Record the teacher's comments as each topic is discussed. Most teachers will be delighted to see you take notes—it's a sign of interest, and helps to assure that what was said will be remembered accurately. The following checklist was prepared by the National Committee for Citizens in Education:

• Is my child performing at grade level in basic skills? Above/below? Math/Reading?

• What achievement, intelligence, or vocational aptitude tests have been given my child in the past year? What do the scores mean?

• What are my child's strengths and weaknesses in major subject areas?

• Can we go over some examples of my child's classwork together?

• Does my child need special help in any academic subject? In social adjustment?

• Would you recommend referral to other school specialists?

- Has my child regularly completed homework you assigned?

- Has my child attended class regularly?

- How well does my child get along with classmates?

- Have you observed any changes in learning progress during the year? Has learning improved or declined dramatically?

- Have you noticed any changes in behavior such as squinting, extreme fatigue or irritability which may be signals of medical problems?

- Would you advise any of the following summer activities: Summer school for remedial help? Enrichment courses? Career related summer job? Home learning activities? A complete rest from school pressures?

- Will you advise any special programs or repeating this grade for next year?

This list of questions, along with other useful bits of information for parents, is available in a handy pocket-size pamphlet entitled *Annual Education Checkup* from The National Committee for Citizens in Education. See Appendix C for the address.

Kids Can Conference Too

Q. When I have conferences with my children's teachers, usually twice a year, my kids always want to go with me. They say it's their right to know what the teacher is saying about them. I have heard that there are teachers in some schools who invite the kids to parent–teacher conferences, but their teachers do not. Do you think it's a good idea for children to attend parent–teacher conferences?

A. The most complete parent–teacher conference will include two kinds of conversations—one about the child and one with the child. The older the child, the more beneficial it is to include him or her in the conference. Certainly there are topics you will wish to discuss alone with the teacher. Such a discussion is in preparation for the conference with your child present. Use these private discussions to exchange and explore your impressions of the child, to clarify uncertainties, and to pinpoint specific areas of concern.

Then, with your child present, proceed as with any regular parent–teacher conference. Discuss his or her achievements and performance levels in the academic areas. Look at samples of his or her work. Discuss his or her strengths, academically and socially. Pinpoint any areas of concern and make specific plans for improvement with your child.

Kids will reap many benefits from being included in such discussions. They'll get a realistic view of themselves as students. They'll see the progress they are making. When they are made part of the planning process they will learn to think about their needs and about the efforts they need to make to improve themselves. Most likely they'll feel more positive about school when they have been listened to and talked with respectfully. There's also a better chance they'll be motivated to carry through on the plans for improvement because they have had a say in formulating them.

If your child will be permitted to attend a conference, it's important for you to have a pre-conference discussion with him. Describe what will be discussed so that he knows what to expect and has a chance to express any concerns that he would like to bring up with the teacher. Have a post-conference discussion, too, to make sure that your child understands what was said and to review and reinforce any plans for change.

Not all schools and/or teachers are open to conferences which include kids. Some resist because any change from established patterns seems upsetting, maybe even risky. Some teachers aren't sure that kids can handle the information being discussed and fear a negative effect on the child. Also, including kids in conferences requires extra time, so a teacher with twenty-five or thirty conferences to schedule may not be willing to make this extra effort. If this is the case in your child's school, it is worthwhile to work for a change in policy. See the introduction to Chapter 9 on page 146 for hints on how to initiate such changes.

Contact Teachers with Concerns

Q.   I attend two parent–teacher conferences for each of my kids every year. Occasionally something comes up between these conferences that I'd like to talk over with the teacher. I hesitate to call, because I know teachers are extremely busy. Do you think it's fair for parents to contact teachers between conferences? If so, is there an established procedure for this?

A.   Yes, it's fair to contact teachers between conferences. In fact, it's unfair *not* to contact them if a real concern or problem arises. Unresolved concerns and persistent problems obstruct learning. The more information teachers have about your kids, the more effectively they can teach them.

Before you contact the teacher, try to sort out the temporary problems from the persistent ones. Wait a few days or a week or two after an incident or concern comes up. Many problems, such as a child expressing dislike of a teacher who has chastised him for a misbehavior, disappear without your interference.

Begin with telephone contact, since this requires less time for both of you. Call during school hours and leave a message for the teacher to call you back or send a note with your child asking the teacher to call you. Don't call the teacher at home after school hours. Teachers need and deserve time away from school concerns.

When the call has been returned, express your concern

and ask the teacher if he or she feels a conference is necessary or if a phone discussion will be adequate.

Legitimate reasons for contacting a teacher between conferences include:

• Your child exhibits a dramatic negative change in attitude towards school, his teacher, his classmates, or his work. This change may be accompanied by physical discomfort: stomach aches, headaches, excessive tiredness, general malaise.

• Your child's academic performance takes a plunge. This plunge may be limited to one subject or may affect all his schoolwork.

• You suspect that the stories your child tells about school may be untrue. Perhaps your child says that there's no spelling instruction. Or he may say that no homework is now being assigned, though all year long there has been homework.

• You notice that your child seems alone and friendless and he complains all of a sudden that no one in his class or school likes him.

• A family problem or crisis has occurred. Perhaps there's been a serious illness or death in the family, or a separation or divorce is pending. Teachers who are aware of these situations in a child's life can offer extra support in school.

• You are planning to take your child out of school for more than a day or two and wish to have assignments for the child to complete while away.

Participate in Parents' Programs

Q. Over the years, I have attended many PTA functions. Frankly, I find many of the programs boring. Paying dues in order to show support for their efforts is one thing, but I do begrudge giving up evenings for the meetings. Is the PTA an outdated organization? Does it serve any function besides raising money for school projects?

A. The secret to making those meetings interesting is getting actively involved. Just paying dues is not enough. Come, listen, participate, take an active part. These are not just women's organizations, either. With men taking a much more active role in parenting nowadays, dads belong inside the school as much as moms.

While fund raising is the most well-known function of parent organizations, much more can be accomplished. These groups often become clearinghouses that can keep you involved and informed on all matters that pertain to your children's education. Sometimes PTA's have a say in major decisions that must be made by the school. Since a group of parents has much more influence than a single parent, any parent wishing to initiate changes in the school should start by talking with PTA officials.

With less federal and state dollars available for education, the traditional fund-raising role is ever more important. Funds are used in a variety of ways, from purchasing computers to supplying band uniforms to supporting summer study for teachers.

The PTA (Parent–Teacher Association) represents the largest parent organization in the country. The local PTA in your school is linked to a state organization which is part of the national organization. When you join your local PTA, you automatically become a member of all three groups. For an additional $8, you can subscribe to *PTA Today,* an excellent magazine that will keep you abreast of all phases of education. A list of other PTA publications is available upon request from the National PTA, 700 N. Rush St., Chicago, IL 60611.

To give you an idea of how far-reaching the aspirations of

the PTA are, below are the five stated objectives of the organization:

1. To promote the welfare of children and youth in home, school, community, and place of worship.
2. To raise the standards of home life.
3. To secure adequate laws for the care and protection of children and youth.
4. To bring into closer relation the home and the school, that parents and teachers may cooperate intelligently in the education of children and youth.
5. To develop between educators and the general public such united efforts as will secure for all children and youth the highest advantages in physical, mental, social, and spiritual education.

Some PTAs, especially in secondary schools, have become PTSAs—parent–teacher–student associations. PTSAs complete the team by having kids, parents, and teachers all working together to improve education for all children. It's a trend that will probably continue.

PTA Dads As stereotyped roles for men and women are discarded, men are increasingly involved in school functions. There is no reason why dads can't become active in the PTA and Parent Advisory Councils. The National PTA recognizes the importance of dad's participation and is urging local chapters to welcome men who wish to become active. In many areas PTA councils have switched to evening meetings to meet the needs of working parents of either sex.

PTOs (Parent–Teacher Organizations) resemble PTAs on the local level, but have no state and national affiliations. Thus their influence on the well-being of all children is more limited.

Many of our state and federal education laws require parent advisory councils. These councils are designed around one specific school program, such as bilingual education, or programs for remedial, handicapped, or gifted students. They make information available to other parents. They give input into major decisions and often have a say in how the dollars are spent. If you have a child in one of these special programs, your involvement with the parent advisory council is one of the best ways to make sure your kid's needs are being met.

Two other organizations exist that provide resources to help parents understand and cope with their child's education.

The National Committee for Citizens in Education (NCCE) is a non-profit public interest organization that helps people gain and use information and skills to influence the quality of public education. Their monthly newspaper, *Network,* provides information on what is happening on the education scene across the country. Their resource catalog offers books, cards, films, products, and services to help improve public schools. For more information, write to NCCE at Suite 410, Wilde Lake Village Green, Columbia, MD 21044.

The Council for Basic Education (CBE) is an organization dedicated to academic excellence in the school. Their monthly newsletter focuses primarily on curriculum, instructional methods, teacher preparation, and teacher evaluation. They also offer publications on a variety of topics. CBE can be reached at 725 Fifteenth Street N.W., Washington, D.C. 20005.

With all the educational issues in which to become involved today, there's no reason for a PTA or any parent organization meeting to be a waste of time. If the organization in your school isn't functioning as well as you would like, don't stay home. Add your talents to the group and work for the necessary changes.

Versatile Volunteers Strengthen Cooperation

Q. Last week when some of my neighbors were over for coffee we were discussing the idea of volunteering in our childrens' schools. Do you think it's a real benefit to the school when parents help out? Whom do we talk to if we decide we want to volunteer?

A. Most schools, especially in these days of declining budgets, welcome any free help from the community they can get. Such volunteer work will benefit you, your child, and the school program. Some schools even have paid or volunteer coordinators who match the interests and talents of parent volunteers with the specific needs expressed by school personnel. They may even provide training where necessary. Call a PTA representative or the school district's administrative office and ask if such a coordinator exists in your school district. If there isn't a coordinator, talk to your child's teacher or the principal of the school.

Volunteering strengthens the relationship between your home and your child's school. Your kids' teachers will get to know you on a friendlier, more informal basis. Because you help them, they'll most likely return the favor by being particularly responsive to your children's needs.

You will benefit personally by volunteering because as a volunteer you will gain a more complete understanding of the school and its programs from the inside. You will also enjoy the good feeling that comes when you give of yourself, your time, and your energies to help others.

Lend a Hand   Join forces with other parents to do a project that will benefit the entire school. The parents of elementary school children in Ithaca, New York, built a creative playground for the kids under the direction of a parent, Mr. Bob Leathers. Other parent groups have planted trees, built bookshelves, raised funds for computer centers, organized book fairs. When teachers and students see such interest and support from the parents, their morale skyrockets.

Your own children will benefit, too. Even though you may not actually be working as a volunteer in their particular classroom, they will feel a sense of pride when you are present in the school. They will feel important. If your time is spent playing learning games with children you'll have learned some activities you can do at home with your own children.

There are many school jobs you might do. Do you like to perform clerical functions, such as collecting lunch money, shelving library books, or running duplicating machines? When the teachers don't have to spend time doing these tasks, they have more time to devote to teaching the children. Would you like to help supervise activities, such as arts and crafts or special projects or playground activities? An extra person is especially welcome when field trips are taken. Maybe you'd prefer to get involved in direct teaching—reading to children or listening to them read, perhaps tutoring a child or two. Being tutored is a very special experience for many children. Tutoring helps academically because it provides extra drill and practice. It often helps just as much emotionally as many children form close relationships with their tutors. When a child is afraid of school, shy, or even hostile, anticipation of the special times alone with you often changes his whole attitude toward himself and his school.

Can a working parent volunteer? Perhaps. You might be able to serve as a resource person, sharing an interest, hobby, or your vocation with the class over a lunch hour. Or you can provide snacks for an evening play, open house, or PTA meeting. How you volunteer and what you do isn't as important as the fact that you are doing it.

If you'd like more information on volunteers in the schools, write the National School Volunteer Program, Inc., 300 N. Washington Street, Alexandria, VA 22312 and ask for their publication, *Volunteers in Education*.

5

••••••••••••••••••••••••••••••••••••

How to Strengthen School Support for Non-Traditional Families

It's August, time for you to register your new stepdaughter at the local school. You greet the principal and the secretary, who gives you a form to fill out. There's a place for parents and guardians to sign, but not for stepparents. You sign anyway. The secretary reads the form, frowns, and says "I'm sorry, but you are not the child's real parent and we cannot register her with just your signature. Please have her real Mom or Dad come to see us."

It's December, and your twins have been unusually moody the last few days. Despite your frequent questions, they've been reluctant to say what's on their minds. Finally one twin blurts out, "I hate school, I'm not going back." After you calm him down, he reveals the problem. The third grade teachers have provided clay for the kids to make Christmas presents for their parents. But each child may make only one gift. Your kids, who must decide which set of parents to make a present for, are caught in an unhappy loyalty conflict.

It's April, and your nine-year-old son arrives home from school in tears. In his hand is a notice of a special father/son dinner and baseball game sponsored by the school. He feels miserable because he knows he can't go—his dad lives in another state.

Family life has changed over the last few decades, a fact too often ignored by schools. Many kids no longer live with two biological parents—instead they live in single parent families, stepfamilies, adoptive families, foster families, and so on. John Naisbitt in *Megatrends* says "the diversity in American households in the 1980's has become a Rubik's cube of complexity. And, like Rubik's cube, the chances of getting it back to its original state are practically nil." Demographers at the Joint Center for Urban Studies of MIT and Harvard, in their report entitled "The Nation's Families 1960–1990," conclude that "these new family models will be with us for a long time, and American families will grow even more diverse."

School involvement now belongs to dad as well as mom, but when dad lives in a different home or perhaps even a different state, staying involved is not a simple task. Even when they live nearby, non-custodial parents often have difficulties being included. Often non-custodial parents do not receive school notices and newsletters by mail. Thus they miss parent-teacher conferences and school events to which they ought to be invited. Sometimes, even though the law guarantees their right, these parents have a difficult time gaining access to their kids' school records.

Many school practices and policies make kids from non-traditional or non-nuclear families seem like second-class citizens. Textbooks still depict the "ideal family" as Mom, Dad, Son, Daughter and the family dog, Spot. School authorization forms rarely leave a place for a stepparent or foster parent to sign. Schools organize special mother/daughter or father/son events, despite the fact that in many cases the appropriate parent is not available. Educators still use terms such as "broken home" to describe situations in which divorce has occured. Such derogatory vocabulary perpetuates negative stereotypes and lowered expectations for these children. Thus many parents from non-traditional homes hesitate to give teachers any family information.

You Can Do It Don't let the bureaucracy of your school intimidate you. On most issues you can find other parents with similar views who will work with you. The school's parent organization can also help. So can the resource groups listed in Appendix 3. All it takes to make changes in programs and policies is one interested parent who is willing to spend the time and energy to make his wishes known to the school community in a cooperative, organized manner.

If a single parent works, the problem is compounded. Many activities, such as conferences and plays, are scheduled during working hours. When events do occur at night, childcare is not always provided, so single parents on a limited budget with no spouse to watch the kids can't attend anyway. If a single parent has early working hours, the kids must be left with a sitter before school. If the sitter is on a different school bus route, kids are often denied access to the bus due to inflexible district policies.

As a parent living in a non-traditional family, you will have to take specific steps to see that your kids' special needs are met.

What You Expect Is What You Get

Q. I'm disturbed by reports that say children whose parents are divorced experience more problems in school than other children. I'm divorced, and my kids aren't causing trouble. Isn't it possible for single or stepparents to raise perfectly normal, well-adjusted children? Do these reports mean that the two-parent nuclear family is the only really acceptable way to raise kids?

A. No evidence clearly states one family structure is better for raising kids than another. What counts in a family is not the family structure but the quality of the relationships and interactions between the family members. Any family structure can provide the quality necessary for raising well-adjusted children. The reports you cite unfortunately cause many parents much needless anxiety and guilt and give rise to negative perceptions and expectations among educators for children from non-nuclear families.

These negative assumptions and expectations tend to become self-fulfilling prophecies. Teachers who expect and perceive problems with an individual or a specific group of kids tend to experience these problems. In addition, when teachers assume that the child's family structure is responsible for his problems, they may shrug their shoulders, take a defeatist attitude, and make no plans to help the child.

If your child experiences difficulties in school, don't let the teacher excuse him on the basis of your divorce or remarriage. Insist that a complete evaluation of the problem be conducted. Each child is an individual with strengths and weaknesses independent of the general tendencies of other children in similar situations. We need to forget categories and labels and instead focus on individual children.

What Teachers Need to Know

Q. Three years ago when I divorced my husband, I hesitated to tell teachers about my marital status because I feared they would stereotype my kids. Now that I am remarried should I let the school know of the changes that have occured in our family?

A. There is a danger that teachers will negatively stereotype your children when they learn of your divorce and remarriage. However, the risks involved when you don't alert teachers to changes in your family probably outweigh this danger.

Most teachers will assume kids live with both biological parents unless told differently. As a result they may unwittingly place kids in unpleasant and embarassing situations. They may make statements like "Go ask your father," only to find that dad lives 1000 miles away. At an open house for families, they may address a stepfather with an incorrect surname. While such incidents may seem like little matters, to kids they can be very important.

Teachers need to know the basic facts about your family, but there is no need to reveal private thoughts and feelings. You do not need to justify your behavior or living situation in any way. Be sure to provide information about where to reach all of the children's parents. Tell them how the adults involved have decided to handle parent conferences and other school functions—whether you can attend peaceably together or need to come to school at separate times.

Keep in mind that non-custodial parents have a legal right to see their child's records. Do not ask the school to withhold any information or to refrain from involving your former spouse in activities. Only a court order can prohibit a parent access to their children's school records. Remember, it's in the best interests of your children for both parents to be involved in the school.

It also helps teachers to know how your kids are adjusting to changes within the family, especially if you see a significant change in your child's behavior or attitude. Such knowledge allows them to be more understanding and supportive of the kids, especially if the kids are going through a difficult period of adjustment.

One of the risks of not being open about family change is that the kids may themselves become secretive about what is happening and withdraw from other kids because they feel "different." A sensitive teacher can help them see that others in the class live in similar situations and that all types of families are okay.

Single Parents Have Needs, Too

Q. As a single parent who works, I find it very difficult to attend school conferences and participate in other parent activities because my pay is docked when I take time off from my job. I'll bet lots of single parents have this problem. Is it reasonable to expect schools to respond to our needs?

A. Too many schools still operate as if the two-parent family with a non-working mom is the norm. A study conducted in 1981 by the National Committee for Citizens in Education entitled "Single Parents and the Public Schools" recommends that schools adopt the following practices to meet the needs of single parents who want to be active in school functions:

• Schedule parent-teacher conferences at times when parents would not have to leave work
• Schedule parent organization meetings in the evening
• Provide child care for young children during parent-teacher conferences and programs or parent organization meetings
• Welcome older children at social events and parent organization meetings
• Initiate a parenting course specifically for single parents.

Join together with other single parents to request that your school initiate these practices. Make the request first to the principal of the school, then to the district superintendent, and finally to the school board if necessary. Ask the local parents' organization to support your efforts.

School people like to remind parents of the positive effect parental involvement has on kids' education. Assure them that when school policies change to make parental involvement more feasible, you'll be happy to become involved.

Trying to be Both Father and Mother Society clings to the notion that the "best" families have a father and mother living in one home with the children. Children living in other family structures are often considered second-class citizens living in less-than-ideal situations. To compensate, the parent with custody often tries to be both mom and dad to the kids. It's difficult to fulfill successfully the role of one parent; it's impossible for one person to perform the job of two. The harder you try to perform as both mom and dad, the more frustrated, harried, and unhappy you will become. Accept reality. One parent is one parent. Do what you can in your role as single parent and encourage the kids to develop their relationship with the non-custodial parent. Children can continue to love both parents while living mostly with one; the kids can become normal, well-adjusted youngsters, too.

Should My Ex-Spouse Attend Conferences with Me?

Q. My ex-husband wants to attend parent–teacher conferences with me. I always feel upset and uptight when he's around, so I'm not sure it's such a good idea. Since he's entitled to know how the kids are doing in school, I don't know if I have the right to tell him he can't be there. What do you suggest?

A. Ideally, divorced parents can attend school conferences and meetings together. A much clearer picture of your child will emerge when both of you are present. Any plans that must be devised to meet your child's specific needs will have both mom's and dad's input. The teacher will appreciate the time saved by not meeting with each parent individually.

However, you should attend together only if everyone can handle the situation comfortably so that the conference remains focused on the kids. When you bring unresolved marital issues and negative emotions to the conference you distract attention from the needs of the children and hinder positive planning.

Sometimes a teacher, because of his or her own thoughts and feelings, is uncomfortable in the presence of divorced parents. If you sense that this will happen, don't attend together. If your child is included in the conference, be sure the child can handle being with both parents at the same time.

Here are some alternatives if you decide not to attend together:

- The teacher holds separate conferences
- The teacher holds conferences with one parent and shares the main points with the other parent by telephone
- The parents take turns attending conferences—one attends in the fall, the other in the spring
- One parent attends the conference and the other gets a copy of report letters or cards in the mail
- One parent attends, takes notes, and shares the information with the other.

If you decide not to attend together because of your discomfort over unresolved issues from the marriage, consider getting some counseling to settle these issues. Think about all the future times you and your ex-spouse may need to be together for the sake of your kids. Everyone concerned, especially the kids, will benefit when divorced parents can see each other and talk together without old issues and feelings getting in the way.

How the Non-Custodial Parent Can Keep Involved

Q. Since my kids live with their mother during the week, I find it difficult to become involved in their schooling. Despite repeated requests, the teacher forgets to send me notices of events for parents. In addition, my ex-wife doesn't want me to attend parent-teacher conferences with her. Should I quit trying to make contact with the school or is my involvement really important to my kids?

A. Keep trying—it may take a great deal of persistence on your part to convince the school that they must cooperate with you. By staying involved with your kids' schooling you demonstrate to them the high value you put upon education. This is bound to exert a positive influence on how they feel about school.

Make it easy for teachers to send you notices of events for parents. Give them a supply of stamped, self-addressed envelopes. Give some to the school secretary, too, in order to receive general school notices as well as class notices. Join the school's parent organization and make sure you are on the mailing list.

Don't force the issue of conferences. Remember that the law guarantees non-custodial parents access to their kids' school records under the provisions of the Family Educational Rights and Privacy Act (FERPA) of 1974. If your district in any way hinders your access to your kids' school records, seek help from the Family Educational Rights and Privacy Act Office, U.S. Department of Education, 4518 Switzer Building, Washington, D.C., 20202.

Give your kids a special bookbag to bring when they visit. Ask them to put samples of their classwork, homework, and art projects in it to share with you. You might even encourage your kids to put some of their textbooks and library books in these bookbags, too. Take the time to look at everything they bring and talk about it with them. You should end up with a clear picture of what they are doing in school. Hang up a bulletin board and choose work and art samples to display each week.

If the kids visit you on school evenings, take responsibility for scheduling the time to complete homework assignments. Don't overstimulate them or keep them up too late—they'll need to be refreshed for school in the morning. If they visit on the weekends, keep these same guidelines in mind. See that they are home early enough Sunday night to have some time to adjust to the change in surroundings before bedtime.

Texts Tell Only One Story

Q. As a stepmother, I'm concerned about the fact that even though my kids and lots of others live in blended families, today's textbooks still portray only the nuclear family. What effect does this stereotyped image of the family have on kids?

A. Over the past twenty years, the image of minorities and women depicted in kids' texts has changed. But the image of the "ideal" family has remained about the same. This stereotype denies kids in other family situations a sense of okayness and belonging. The kids often feel left out and second-class. They infer that their families somehow aren't as good because they have been excluded from the texts.

To counteract this image, discuss the subject with your kids. Explain that years ago, the majority of families contained a mom, dad, and their biological kids. Tell them it takes time for the folks who publish the texts to catch up with the changes in society. Assure them that all types of families are OK. Perhaps even discuss some family structures with which they may not be familiar.

> **Authorization Forms** Do you know that stepparents have no legal relationship to their children? In times of medical emergencies, this becomes a serious matter. Should a stepchild require treatment when neither biological parent is available to sign an authorization form, a stepparent may not automatically sign in their absence. To avoid such situations, it makes sense for the biological parents to give stepparents legal written permission to authorize emergency medical treatment for their children.

Library books have done a better job depicting different family types than textbooks. Ask the librarian at the school or public library to help you find these books. Read them with your kids and discuss the differences between textbooks and library books in the portrayal of families.

Next, let the teachers, administrators, curriculum specialists, members of the textbook selection committee (if there is one), and school board members all know your concerns. Ask them to be careful that the books they choose in the future depict different family structures. You'll have more clout if you join forces with other similarly concerned parents.

Write letters to let the publishers know your concerns. It won't help your kids this year or next, but eventually the publishers will get the message and make the necessary changes. Other kids will benefit because you cared enough to take action.

Holiday Hassles

Q. I'm dreading the holidays again this year because it's always such a difficult time for my two kids. Since both their father and I have remarried, the kids have two mothers and two fathers. They become very upset when, for example, they are given time and materials to make a present for one dad but not for two. I don't think it's fair for them to have to choose between parents. With so many divorced and remarried families, couldn't the schools deal with the holidays differently?

A. Given the large number of non-nuclear families, it's surprising how many schools and teachers still force kids to choose between parents. Some teachers do this out of ignorance of kids' home situations, others because they mistakenly hope to spare the kids some embarrassment.

Traditionally holidays are times of family celebrations, particularly Thanksgiving, Christmas and Chanukah, Mother's Day, and Father's Day. The answer is not for teachers to ignore the holidays because some children live in different family situations. Rather, holidays are a great opportunity for schools to help all children become aware of different family structures.

Treating children from different types of families should be no different from treating children from different ethnic and racial backgrounds. The emphasis should be that we are all different and that being different is OK.

The best way to sensitize teachers to the needs of your kids at holiday time is to have the parents' organization in your school schedule a panel discussion on this topic. Include parents, teachers, and community resource people on the panel. Perhaps some older students who have encountered these difficulties would be willing to talk about their experiences. The recommendations of the panel should be written up and distributed to all school personnel. Place a copy in your school's teacher handbook if one exists. If such a program can't be organized, have a group of parents and interested teachers meet and draw up a list of recommendations to be distributed in the same manner.

It won't hurt to have an individual talk with your kids'

teachers, too. Include the kids in the talk. This personal contact may help the teacher understand your kids' needs on a deeper level.

Discussing Divorce During the Day

Q. The school counselor has invited my ten- and twelve-year-old sons to join a weekly group where kids discuss how they feel about their parents' divorce. I'm uncertain about the idea. To begin with, neither boy is a terrific student. I'm afraid missing time from classroom instruction just to talk with a group of kids will interfere with their learning. I'm also not sure I like the idea of their discussing family problems in front of other kids who might spread the information around the neighborhood. Isn't divorce something parents and families should deal with by themselves, without interference from the school?

A. Certainly the job of helping children deal with separation and divorce rests primarily on parental shoulders. Yet the school can supplement the efforts of parents and provide additional support unique to the school setting.

While most adults are aware of the high rate of divorce today, many children of divorce are unaware that many of their classmates face the same home situation and experience similar feelings and reactions. Being part of a group shows children that they are not alone. A real sense of support, comfort, and belonging blossoms when they talk and share similar life experiences with other children.

All children who have experienced divorce need to learn to deal with the feelings that accompany this change in their lives. Often children are frightened and confused by the intensity of their feelings, and by the variety of feelings they experience. Youngsters need the chance to vent these feelings, to sort them out and to accept them as normal. Ideally, this can be done with the help of a sympathetic parent, but the school counselor is also in a strong position to help. Since the counselor is uninvolved personally it's often easier for him to listen and to react objectively to the child. Children may also feel freer to talk about their negative feelings with an outsider. This protects the parents from having to confront their child's difficulties at a time when the adults are working out their own personal problems. Hearing other children express their feelings can help a child who denies his own pain to become aware of and accept his personal feelings.

Settle the Past Unlike many marriages, most divorces last forever. For the sake of your kids, make sure your divorce works well. Kids can't concentrate in school when divorced parents are still fighting. They need their parents to be able to attend school functions together without hidden hostility oozing forth. If there are unsettled issues, consider getting professional help to resolve them. Your kids' school success depends on it.

Besides getting a chance to explore their feelings, your boys will learn everyday coping skills. Youngsters might gain specific communication skills or find ways to stay close to a parent who no longer lives nearby. They may learn how to react to their "at home" parent who may be tired and grouchy from working all day and doing household chores all evening. They may learn steps to take when they feel lonely or unhappy.

Their academic skills will probably not suffer from the missed classroom time. Usually such a group requires only thirty minutes once or twice a week. Indeed their grades are likely to go down if they cannot learn the skills they need to cope with their feelings. Kids will have difficulty concentrating on studies when home and personal problems are pressing.

School counselors report that few kids talk outside the

group about what goes on during the sessions. Confidentiality is stressed and those who violate this code of conduct are excluded from the group. In fact, kids generally respect the confidentiality rule so well that some parents report frustration because their child refuses to discuss what happens in the group with them. Children are free to tell their parents about their participation in the group, but not about anyone else's contributions.

Children who can both talk to a sympathetic parent and participate in a school group hold the best chances of adjusting to divorce in a healthy way.

Should you decide to remarry someday, a stepfamily discussion group would be equally helpful to your boys.

6

•••••••••••••••••••••••••••••••••

How to Overcome
Academic Problems

Report cards arrived with the children this afternoon. Normally
you'd be pleased when your child shows all "B's." But this
time the teacher's comment that he "could do better if he tried
more" worries you. Does this child have an academic problem
that needs your attention or is he just lazy? Another child has
"B's" and "C's," yet the teacher says "he is working to capacity." Does that mean your child is a slow learner, a child with
limited abilities? A third child, always a very good student, has
lower marks in most subjects this semester. "What's going
on?" you wonder. What should you do to make sure that next
time his marks are high?

Your youngest, in first grade, was marked "satisfactory"
in all subjects except reading, which is marked "unsatisfac-

tory." The teacher says, "Don't worry. Your daughter is just immature and will catch on eventually." You are not so sure. Her former kindergarten teacher also called her "immature," so apparently nothing has changed over the last twelve months. What if she remains immature? Will she fail and have to repeat first grade? If there is a problem, couldn't something be done now to help her before she fails?

Recognizing Academic Problems

Most children are bound to experience some kind of academic difficulty at some point during the thirteen years of elementary and secondary schooling. With some kids, the difficulty extends to all areas of schoolwork. With others, it's limited to one or two subjects.

Be alert for clues that your child might be experiencing academic difficulties. Don't assume that if you don't hear from a teacher, all is well with your kids. While you can expect teachers to eventually contact you if they spot a problem, they may not do so until after your child has experienced a good deal of failure. Teachers have a lot of children to deal with each day, which makes it difficult to spot individual problems quickly. During the early part of the school year, teachers won't know your children well enough to know if their performance is deteriorating. Don't assume that if you don't hear from a teacher, all is well with your kids. Be alert for clues that your child might be experiencing academic difficulties.

Report card grades are an obvious clue, but they only come two to four times a year. Standardized test scores are generally available only once a year.

Marks on homework and test papers come more frequently, so encourage your kids to show them to you and talk about their papers frequently. Do this weekly with kids in the lower grades and at least once a month with older kids. Look for grades that seem lower than usual over a few weeks and listen for expressions of on-going difficulties and frustration with a subject.

Listen to what your child has to say about school at other times. Occasionally steer the dinnertime conversation around to teachers, subjects, learning. Do any specific complaints come up over and over again? Sometimes kids express academic problems indirectly. They say they are bored or don't like the teacher or school in general. Kids' gripes, when they persist for a few weeks, coupled with your observations of schoolwork brought home, may point to an academic problem.

Watch for behavioral changes. A kid who is suddenly whiney, moody, aggressive, or withdrawn may be experiencing academic problems. Physical symptoms may also appear, including stomach aches, headaches and general fatigue, and listlessness.

Identifying Causes of Academic Problems

It's important to deal with both the symptoms and the causes of academic problems. The questions and answers found later in this chapter deal with how to alleviate the symptoms, the actual academic difficulties. In this section, let's explore the most common causes for academic difficulties and make suggestions about how to eliminate them.

Beware of very simplistic, unspecific terms often used to define the causes of academic problems. Sometimes teachers label kids "lazy," "unmotivated," "underachieving," "immature." These terms are not helpful and confuse the picture. Labels get in the way of the search for more accurate identification, and thus delay appropriate corrective action.

Here are the seven most common causes of academic difficulties:

1. Your child has limited academic ability and potential.

2. Your child has a neurological problem, which is sometimes referred to as a learning disability.
3. Your child has a medical problem, such as poor eyesight and/or hearing, allergies, glandular malfunctions, etc.
4. Your child has an emotional or psychological problem. This may be a long-standing problem or it may be a temporary reaction to an unusually stressful situation at home or at school.
5. Your child has been placed in an ineffective learning situation. He may have a poor teacher or the methods and materials used for instruction may be inappropriate.
6. Your child puts forth little effort because he fears mistakes and failure.
7. Your child chooses to perform poorly in order to get extra attention, engage you or the teacher in power struggles, or get revenge.

It's possible that your child's academic problems are rooted in more than one of these causes. It may take some time to discover which cause or causes are affecting your child. You'll need to enlist the cooperation of your child, his teacher, and possibly other professionals in reaching a complete and accurate diagnosis.

Start with a school conference, because everyone who works with your child needs to get a clear picture of his problems and concerns. Be sure to include your child at least part of the time. Use this conference to make a plan for gathering the data to be used in pinpointing the cause and in analyzing the learning problems. Part of the evaluation process must include a specific diagnosis of your child's subject area strengths and weaknesses. After the plan has been completed, you'll need to meet again to review the data and decide what steps to take to solve the problem.

Plan to gather as much data as possible. School professionals can test for academic achievement and potential, strengths and weaknesses, and learning styles. The school nurse can usually test vision and hearing acuity. In addition, a complete physical by your child's pediatrician is always a good idea, especially if it's been a while since the last check-up.

Uncovering emotional problems begins with observations of your child's behavior by you at home and the teachers at school. Any changes in patterns? Is he moody, irritable, withdrawn, aggressive? Both parents need to spend time individually with him, discussing how he feels about himself, his school, his friends, his family, and so forth. Often, when he is away from school and family, a child may feel freer to say what's on his mind. If you sense there is an emotional problem but your child refuses to talk about it, ask the school counselor or psychologist to interview your child. You are not looking for counseling at this point; rather, you want to know whether they perceive any emotional problems.

You Could Do Better Resist telling your child "You could do better." While you might hope these words will encourage your kids to put forth greater efforts, often the opposite effect is true. Kids translate "You could do better" into "I'm not good enough," or "No matter what I do it isn't good enough," or even into "I can't ever please Mom or Dad." To encourage greater efforts, first give them approval of what they have done. Then ask them if they are satisfied with the results of their efforts. Use their comments to lead into a discussion of what they might do differently if faced with the same task or situation another time.

Finding out if the problem is due to a poor teaching situation is tricky. No teacher will tell you that he or she is not doing a good job. Other school professionals will hesitate to point the finger. So you will have to evaluate this from your own impressions. Talk to the teacher. Talk to your child. Talk to other parents whose children have been assigned to the same teacher. Have a confidential talk with the local PTA officials, too. Unfortunately, you may feel you are up against a conspiracy of silence. No one likes to admit that poor teachers exist, even though everyone knows they do.

How will you know if your child's academic problems are caused by his desire for extra attention, power, revenge, or avoidance of failure? Check all the above possibilities first, for this area is less tangible and harder to diagnose. Unfortunately, there's no test that pinpoints a child's mistaken perceptions of how to get along. Carefully observe when your child misbehaves at home. Use your feelings and reactions as a guide. If your child misbehaves as a way to gain extra attention, you will find yourself feeling irritated and annoyed, and you will tend to coax, prod, and nag him to do better. If power is what your child is seeking, your feelings will be much stronger—anger and frustration will replace the irritation and annoyance. Your initial reaction to his behavior will most likely be attempts to force him to behave differently. If revenge is your child's motivation for misbehavior, then feelings of hurt and disappointment are added to the anger and frustration and you may find yourself wanting to get even in return. Your feelings won't be as negative as the ones above if your child misbehaves to avoid failure. More likely you'll feel confused, helpless, and baffled, and you'll wonder what's wrong with your child. Become aware of how often such behaviors occur around the house.

Then discuss your observations with the teacher and school counselor and ask them to notice how your child behaves in school in non-academic situations. See if they notice behaviors that result in similar feelings and reactions on their part. The greater the frequency of attention-getting, power, revenge, and avoidance of failure behaviors in all areas of a child's life, the stronger the suspicion that these behaviors contribute to academic problems.

Planning Solutions to Academic Problems

Once all the data is collected, it's time for a conference to look at the information and to plan solutions. Steps need to be taken to remediate both the symptoms and the causes of the difficulty.

The school professionals have the responsibility to suggest and implement specific steps to overcome any academic weakness while they build upon your child's strengths. They may choose to change the classroom program by using a different method of teaching or by including supplementary materials. They may suggest additional practice sessions for your child, alone or in a group, taught by an aide, volunteer, or remedial reading teacher. They may wish to place your child in a special school program for kids experiencing academic difficulties. You may be asked to supervise specific drill and reinforcement activities at home, under the teachers' direction.

If the cause of the problem appears to be mainly low ability or a learning disability, such a change in the teaching program may be all that's necessary. If you feel that the cause is poor teaching, these changes might be all that's needed to help your child. Wait and see what happens. If you see no positive results and you still feel that poor teaching is the cause, then it's time to think about asking for a change of teacher. Because such a change disrupts your child's entire program, exhaust every other possible route first.

If a medical problem has been discovered, the doctor should prescribe what needs to be done to alleviate the problem. It will be your job to pay particular attention to any dietary suggestions that are made and to administer any prescribed medication properly.

Emotional problems and difficulties caused by fear of failure can be alleviated with the help of a counselor, psychologist, or psychiatrist. Some schools have counselors or psychologists who do group counseling sessions with kids. More likely, however, you will need to seek help for emotional problems outside of school. Contact either a local agency such as Mental Health or Family Service or a private practitioner. The school may be able to refer you to someone. PTA officials might also be able to give you a reference. Some counselors involve parents, and even siblings, in working out the problems of the child. So be prepared to stay involved.

You can help alleviate fear of failure behaviors, too. Relax any pressure you put on your kids to achieve and show them that you expect mistakes as they learn. Teachers can help by making small changes in the school program. Perhaps the teacher can assign tasks in smaller segments, give more frequent feedback, and allow the child to repeat tasks done correctly. Class discussions about how mistakes are part of the learning process are useful, too. When teachers allow kids to talk about their mistakes and their plans for correcting these mistakes in the future, the kids' fears of making mistakes are greatly decreased. Feel free to make these suggestions to the teacher during the conference.

Problems related to attention, power, and revenge behaviors require the concentrated efforts of all adults involved with your child, both at home and at school. When the child is engaging in attention-getting behavior, decrease the amount of attention given for academic difficulties while greatly increasing the attention given at all other times. Ask him what went well in school today. Did he have fun with a friend on the playground? Draw a picture he likes in art class? Enjoy listening to a story? When looking at the worksheets he brings home, ignore the correction and comment on the things he did well. The goal is to help your child see that he gains more attention for success than for failure. Ask the teacher to help find ways that the child can receive recognition for accomplishments during the school day while the family does the same at home.

If the child's behavior is a play for power, sidestep this behavior and make learning contracts that allow some choices and have built-in consequences, both positive and negative, depending on how your child carries through with the choices. These learning contracts need to be made during a conference between the teacher, parents, and child. A neutral person, such as a counselor or the school principal, may be a helpful facilitator.

Repeating Academic Successes   "Motivation to improve is the product, not the source of achievement," states Benjamin Bloom in his book *All Our Children Learning*. Being reminded of past achievements motivates kids to seek further success. Allow your children to feel the full benefit of their academic achievements, no matter how great or small, by having them repeat their accomplishments over and over again. A story your child has learned to read can be read aloud any number of times—to you, to relatives, to younger children who live nearby, even to a tape recorder which plays back his success. Make up math problems that you know your child can do and let him do these over and over. The same goes for spelling words. The more academic difficulties your child experiences in school, the more ways you must find for him to demonstrate and repeat every skill he has acquired.

If he is attempting to get revenge he needs a similar learning contract. In addition, it would be advisable to find out why the child feels a need to get even. A counseling professional will be most helpful here.

No matter what the cause of the academic problem, the solution needs to emphasize the encouragement and motivation techniques discussed in Chapter 3. Review these frequently so that you become more and more skillful in their application.

Mom Suspects a Reading Problem

Q. I have a son in third grade who doesn't read very well. Last night he brought home the reading book he is using in school this year and it was painful listening to him trying to read a story about astronauts. He stumbled along, making mistake after mistake. His teacher last year said I shouldn't worry, that he was just slow in developing, and that sooner or later he'd catch up to the other kids. I'm not so sure. Even though his report card grades are average, I'm wondering if he has some kind of reading disability that requires special help. How can I find out?

A. You are wise to suspect your son's problem may be more than just a developmental slowness or lateness. As stated earlier in this chapter, don't accept simplistic explanations for difficulties. If you wait much longer to have an evaluation made to see if he has a reading disability, he may experience so much frustration with reading that he either turns off to school completely or becomes a discipline problem.

All schools are mandated by law to evaluate any child who is suspected of having a learning disability. This mandate for evaluation is part of a law entitled "Education for All Handicapped Children," also known as PL 94-142. Don't let the word "handicapped" throw you. It is not synonymous with retarded, as many parents fear. There are many different types of handicaps that appear in all gradations of severity. Some are severe enough to require children to attend special schools designed to serve their special needs, while other, milder handicaps allow the child to remain in his regular classroom but entitle him to receive at least an hour each day of specialized instruction from a teacher certified in special education or reading.

To start the evaluation process, make an appointment to talk to either the principal of your son's school or the special education administrator in your school district. Tell him or her that you suspect that your son has a handicapping condition and you want an evaluation. Bring along a request for the evaluation in writing and date the letter. You must use the words "handicapping condition" because the school is mandated to evaluate children with suspected handicapping conditions but not children with "ordinary" reading problems.

This evaluation should include data on academic performance, general intelligence, physical coordination, and vision and hearing abilities. The data will be compiled by a team of different teachers and specialists. The task of this team is to gather and evaluate all data, and to plan an individualized education for your son if, indeed, a handicapping condition such as a learning disability exists and can be documented according to the legal guidelines stated in PL 94-142.

By law, this committee cannot officially meet without notifying you of meetings and requesting your presence. You have the right to see and keep copies of all test data, to participate in the interpretation of the data, and in the formulation of a special plan to meet your son's learning needs that is called an Individualized Educational Program (IEP). If you disagree with the findings, or the plan that is formulated, you are entitled to request a special hearing with an impartial examiner, who will then make the final decision concerning your child's program.

All of these legalities and formalities can become very confusing. If you encounter difficulty anywhere along the line, call an officer of your local PTA and find out if there is an advocacy group in your area for parents of children with learning problems. If there is no such group, you can contact the National Association for Children with Learning Disabilities, 4156 Library Road, Pittsburgh, PA 15234, an excellent organization with branches throughout the country. If you want more detailed information on the laws concerning children's educational rights, write to the Children's Defense Fund, 122 C Street N.W., Washington, D.C. 20001 and ask for the handbook entitled "94-142 and 504: Numbers That Add Up to Educational Rights for Handicapped Children."

What Should an Evaluation Include?

Q. I have signed permission for my daughter's academic problems to be tested and evaluated. What kinds of tests will she be given and how will I know what these tests mean?

A. A complete evaluation tests four areas: potential learning ability, achievement, skill mastery, and learning style. Many schools administer group tests in at least the first three areas to all children each year, so some test data describing your daughter may already exist. When academic difficulties are evaluated, additional individual testing is necessary. Group testing is not accurate or precise enough to pinpoint specific difficulties correctly. Individual testing may be done by the classroom teacher, a specialist in reading, learning disabilities or special education, a psychologist, or a combination of these.

Tests of potential learning ability are often referred to as intelligence tests. These tell you approximately how well your child should be able to perform in school. Schools prefer to tell parents the range of their child's ability, rather than a single IQ number which may be misleading. You will be told whether your daughter has low, low average, average, high average, or superior ability.

Achievement tests tell you how well your child is performing in relation to the standards for her grade and to other similar students. You will be told a grade equivalent score, such as 3.2. The first number indicates the school grade level, the second the school month. So 3.2 means that your child's reading level is third grade, second month. 7.6 means that her reading level is seventh grade, sixth month. Compare this figure to your child's actual grade to see whether it is the same, higher or lower and you'll be able to judge your child's performance level.

You may also be given a percentile score. This score tells you how well your child performs compared to other kids her age. If your child scores in the twenty-ninth percentile, all kids in the thirtieth percentile and above scored better; those below the twenty-ninth percentile scored worse. For the child scoring in the seventy-eighth percentile, seventy-seven percent of the kids received lower scores; twenty-one percent received higher scores.

Do not take the scores on these tests as absolutes. There are many factors that affect your child's performance such as the amount of sleep she got the night before the tests, the noise and distractions present during the tests, her performance anxiety, the skill of the tester, etc. Some of the problems are in the tests themselves. For example, there is no nationwide agreement on which reading or math skills should be taught in which grade, so different schools teach skills in different sequences. If your school has a sequence different from the one used to construct the test, your child may score badly even though she does very well in school.

The skill-mastery tests are designed to pinpoint which skills your daughter has mastered and which she has not. These tests are usually directly related to the classroom instructional materials and give a fairly accurate picture of specific strengths and weaknesses. Results of these tests are presented as checklists.

Children have different styles of learning and ways of processing information. Several tests may be needed to identify your daughter's particular style. Then an instructional program matched to her style can be set up.

As you can see, no one test gives the complete story.

When a School Doesn't Give Grades

Q. My kids bring home report letters instead of report cards. These letters describe what the kids are doing in reading, math, spelling, etc. I am frustrated by these letters because they don't have grades on them. Without an A, B, or C, I can't really tell how well my kids are doing compared to others in their classes. I also can't tell if they are learning all that's required to pass into the next grade. Why do some schools send report letters instead of grades and how can I tell from these letters if my child has an academic problem?

A. Many educators feel that these letters tell you much more than just a simple letter grade. A typical report letter consists of a description of your child's performance, a checklist of skills mastered, and, usually, a comment about the child's progress since the last time a report letter was sent. Letter grades give you only the teacher's rather arbitrary evaluation of how he feels your child has performed. It doesn't point out strengths and weaknesses or specific skills.

Many parents prefer letter grades simply because that's what they are used to from their own school days. They know they can be happy with A's, fairly pleased with B's and probably upset with C's and angry with D's and F's. They know a child experiencing many C's and below is having academic problems. They can easily compare this term's grade to last term's grade and their kids with their neighbor's kids. It's much easier to brag about a kid with straight A's than a kid with all the skills checked on the mastery list.

Most report letters will tell you the grade level of your child's performance. They will also note whether or not he is experiencing academic problems that need special attention. If your letter doesn't do this to your satisfaction, write the teacher a note with your specific questions. Is my child performing at grade level in each subject? Do you expect him to master all the skills necessary for promotion to the next grade? Do you perceive any academic problems that need remediation, either at school or at home? Ask the teacher to answer on the same sheet and return it to you, or to give you a call one afternoon to discuss your questions. You have a right to these answers if you can't find them in the original report letter.

What's in a Name?

Q. How damaging are the labels a school puts on a child? My son needs special help for a learning disability problem. In order to receive these special services, his teacher told us he must be officially designated "learning disabled" and that this label will appear on his school records. We want him to have the extra help, but not the label. Is it legal for the school to refuse remedial services unless a child is labeled?

A. Danger always exists when children are labeled. Labels themselves generally describe symptoms, not causes. Unfortunately, labels are often used as explanations for a problem, and the underlying causes are not adequately explored and remediated.

Perhaps the biggest danger of labeling children is that expectations for their performance might be lowered. Parents and teachers may start to treat the kids as if they were disabled in all areas instead of in just the affected area. Studies have shown that lower adult expectations result in poorer child performance. The problem gets worse when the kids tune in to these adult expectations and learn to see themselves as incapable. A label can then become a self-fulfilling prophecy. When we call people handicapped, we treat them as if they are, they come to believe they are, and then they act accordingly.

Labels focus on people's weaknesses. Strengths get ignored, and often disappear as a result. Self-confidence lowers when the "I can'ts" become more of a focus than the "I can's."

In our school systems, labels are often mandated by state and federal guidelines as prerequisites for special services in an attempt to contain costs. Since remediation of academic problems by special teachers is an expensive proposition, most districts are anxious to limit the numbers of students served. Thus it is legal for districts to label kids based on the results of special testing and to deny services to kids who don't qualify or whose parents refuse the labels.

Non-Academic Successes Children struggling with academic difficulties need lots of success experiences elsewhere in their lives. Encourage their non-academic interests and talents. Give more attention and recognition to their achievements in these areas than you do to the academic problems. Allow them to join with others who share similar hobbies. Make sure that their teachers are aware of special interests and talents; clever teachers know how to use these as a basis for reading, writing, and arithmetic practice.

If your son needs the remediation, don't deny him the program because of the label. Rather, take steps to minimize the dangers described above. Make sure that everyone involved, including your child, is aware of his strengths and places a good deal of importance and attention on them. Do not lower standards or expectations in any area except the one directly affected by the disability. Don't overprotect your child or try to compensate for the disability by being unduly lenient in discipline matters. Avoid pity.

Read aloud stories of famous people who had problems early in their school careers and who went on to become famous in their fields and made important contributions to the world. Albert Einstein and Nelson Rockefeller are two names that come to mind quickly. Your school or local librarian can suggest many more similar biographies.

Reluctance to Use the Resource Room

Q. My daughter is supposed to go to the resource room for one hour each afternoon for remedial reading instruction. She doesn't want to go. She says that because she gets special help other kids tease her and call her "stupid." She also complains that it's unfair for her to have to do all the work in the classroom and all the work in the resource room. Should I insist that she go despite her reluctance?

A. Your daughter was assigned to the resource room because she needs additional specialized reading instruction to improve her reading skills. Resource room teachers have been trained in either remedial reading or special education, are assigned fewer students, and have access to additional instructional materials. No classroom teacher can provide such individualized instruction. So, yes, if testing has shown that your daughter needs resource room instruction, you should insist that she attend.

Take steps to overcome your daughter's reluctance. Begin by listening to all her feelings about going to the resource room. Your goal is to let her know that you understand the difficult dilemma she is in and will provide your support as she solves her problem.

Avoid commiserating with her about how terrible the situation is. Difficult, yes, but miserable, no. Give her the message that being in a difficult situation is OK and that she can learn to handle it. Also let her know that sometimes she'll have to do some things that she dislikes. We can learn even if we don't particularly like the situation in which we find ourselves.

Sidestep the "unfairness" trap. Most people equate fairness with treating everyone the same. Yet kids are not all the same—they have different abilities and different needs, so they need different programs. Yes, some kids have to do more work than other kids in order to learn the same amount. That's simply a fact of life. No use arguing the point.

Next, schedule a conference between the classroom and resource room teachers, yourself, and your daughter. It's important for the teachers to be aware of your daughter's reluctance and to help find solutions to overcome it. Below are a few possible steps to take; use the conference to brainstorm other possibilities.

Make sure that when it's time to go to the resource room your daughter leaves her regular class with a minimum of attention focused on her. Avoid having the teacher call her name to tell her it's time to go. If she can tell time, give her the responsibility of quietly leaving the classroom on time. If she can't, give her a picture of a clock with the hands pointed to the correct time. When the hands of the clock on the wall match the hands of the clock on her picture, she can leave.

Use this conference time to plan how missed classroom work will be handled. This work may have to be modified to suit your daughter's reading level. She may need some extra instruction from the teacher to complete it. Perhaps a classmate could act as a special tutor when your daughter returns from the resource room. It may be necessary for you to provide some specific help at home, under the teacher's direction. Having a plan should ease your daughter's anxieties about the classroom work.

When your daughter sees improvement in her reading skills, she will be more enthusiastic about the extra work. Ask the resource room teacher to show your daughter her gains on a weekly basis. Some teachers keep lists of skills to be mastered and check them off one by one as the child improves. Your daughter should see this list and be the one to check things off. Then she can see what she has already learned and what is left to learn. Some teachers have the kids keep a file box of words they have mastered. As the file grows thicker and thicker, kids can actually see and feel what they have learned. Your daughter might also keep lists of books she can now read. Talk to her about her new skills, words, and books, so your daughter knows that you are aware of, and proud of, her achievements.

It's the classroom teacher's job to deal with the taunts from other children. He needs to do some consciousness-raising with the whole class about individual differences and name-calling. The teacher should do this in a general way, as part of the curriculum, without specifically calling attention to your daughter.

Tutoring in School

Q. I've received a note from my daughter's teacher that she has been assigned a special volunteer tutor for extra help in arithmetic. They want my signature on the note saying I agree to the tutoring. Should I sign it? Does special tutoring do much good?

A. Many schools rely on volunteer tutors to provide extra help for kids who need it. Before you give permission, there are several questions you should ask to make sure that the tutoring your child will receive will be effective. If the answers don't convince you that the tutoring will be beneficial to your daughter, make an appointment to discuss the matter with her teacher.

First find out who the tutor will be. Ask who will train, supervise, and provide materials for the tutor. Make sure that the tutor will not be teaching new skills, but rather reinforcing skills already taught. Teaching new skills is the job of the professional teacher.

The next question is how often the tutoring sessions will occur. To have a positive effect on classroom performance, your child will need a minimum of two or three sessions per week. Less then that just doesn't accomplish much. Short, frequent sessions get the best results.

Next you will want to know what time during the day the tutoring sessions are scheduled. What will your daughter be missing in the classroom? The tutoring should not conflict with instructional periods with the teacher; otherwise, your daughter will be getting practice with one skill but will fall behind in another. If the session occurs during independent work time, find out if any modification of classroom requirements for your daughter will be made. If she is not able to finish independent work because of the tutoring and has to miss playground time or gym to complete assignments, then the tutoring is not helpful.

Ask where your daughter and the tutor will work. A quiet library or learning center is best. Some overcrowded schools use hallways; this distracts both the child and the tutor.

If you are satisfied with the answers to the above questions, give your permission. The extra practice can be very beneficial to your daughter. In addition, most tutors are warm, friendly, caring people and their visits often become the highlight of a child's day, something special just for them that breaks up the school routine.

After-School Academics

Q. I'm trying to decide whether or not to send my ten-year-old for private tutoring two days a week. He took part in a summer reading program and the director of that program recommends that he continue after school. Are classes after 3:00 P.M. too much for a kid?

A. Before deciding whether or not to continue the tutoring, you need more information.

First, find out how far behind his grade level your son is reading and what plans his school will make for giving him remedial help. Some schools have extensive remedial reading programs where kids receive extra instruction in small groups taught by specialized reading teachers or aides. Sometimes all a school provides is extra instruction a few times a week with a community volunteer or extra reading assignments to be completed at home under the supervision of a parent.

If your son is more than one year behind his grade level,

he'll progress fastest if he receives extra instruction two or three times a week by a trained reading teacher or aide. If the school can't provide this, then continuing the summer program would be a good idea. A tutoring center can provide more specific instruction and trained supervision than you can at home. You'll also avoid the power struggles that often occur when parents try to supervise assignments at home.

Before a decision is made you also need to know how your son feels about it; his attitude and motivation will directly influence the outcome of any remedial program. If he wants to go, if he's feeling successful at the tutoring center, then by all means continue, even if the school is providing adequate remedial services. If a child is eager and willing to accept that help, there is no such thing as too much. If your son is negative about continuing at the center, it just won't work. It will do more harm than good. If going to the center makes him feel like a failure and puts too much pressure on him, it's time to stop.

Remember When? Kids feel encouraged when they can see their academic progress. Help them do this by pointing out skills they have today that they didn't have yesterday. Ask them frequently, "Remember when you couldn't read this story? Remember when you couldn't spell this word? Remember when you couldn't multiply 7×9?" Ask them occasionally what they know today that they didn't know yesterday, last week, last month. Look to the future, too, and ask them what they think they'll know tomorrow that they don't know today.

If you decide to continue the tutoring, find out how that program will be coordinated with the school program. The better coordinated the two programs are, the more success your son will experience. Ideally, there should be periodic conferences between all the teachers involved with your son's reading.

Be sure to set the tutoring schedule so that it doesn't conflict with your son's favorite after-school activities.

When Test Scores Are High and Grades Are Poor

Q. My daughter brings home poor report cards, yet her scores on tests are almost always above 90. Her teacher says that she gives my daughter poor grades because she fails to turn in her homework. My daughter refuses to do much homework, saying she already understands the material and doesn't need to practice. I feel like I'm in the middle of a battle between my daughter and her teacher. Do you think my daughter might have some hidden academic problem?

A. Your daughter's grades apparently do not reflect either her ability or her achievement. They reflect her unwillingness to accept the authority of her teacher. She is, in a sense, being penalized for being bright, for thinking for herself, and for trying to control her own learning experiences. Some children do need homework to practice and reinforce skills taught during the day. Your daughter, as her test scores show, does not. So it seems as if her problem has more to do with a misplaced power struggle than with academics.

Arrange a conference with your daughter and her teacher to explore solutions to the homework problem. If the teacher is willing, the easiest solution is to give your daughter a different type of homework. Instead of reinforcement, it sounds as if she needs enrichment activities that allow her to extend her learning. Probably your daughter can suggest homework activities that would stimulate and excite her.

Sometimes teachers are reluctant to make exceptions for one child. They fear that if they make special arrangements for one child, they will have to do it for many. They worry about losing control or taking on too much extra work. Sympathize with the teacher's difficulty, but emphasize your child's needs and press for a solution that seems workable for all.

Reasons for Repeating

Q. My son is in third grade, but reads on a first grade level according to his teacher. She says the best way to help him with his reading problems is to have him repeat third grade next year. I'm worried that not being promoted will cause him to feel like a failure which will make him do worse, not better, next year. Is repeating a grade a good solution to academic difficulties?

A. Sometimes, yes, more often, no. Repeating a grade is only one possible solution to academic problems and is appropriate only for certain students in specific situations.

Repeating a grade may be helpful to a child experiencing difficulties in all academic areas. If social and/or emotional problems also exist, the case for repeating the grade is even stronger. Repeating also can be beneficial when a complete diagnosis of the child's educational needs has been made and it appears that the repeated program will meet the child's demonstrated needs. Finally, repeating a grade will be successful only if the parents and the child can accept and support the idea, and are able to plan carefully to combat the feelings of frustration and failure that generally occur when a child repeats a grade.

Do not even consider allowing your child to repeat a grade unless a complete diagnosis has been made of his educational needs and the cause of his problems has been identified. Disregard simplistic terms such as "immature" and "unmotivated" that tell you nothing specific about your child and press for a detailed evaluation.

Repeating a grade taught by the same methods and materials probably won't help your child much. Your child didn't learn the first time with these materials—chances are, he won't learn the second time. Schools can modify the instructional program in many ways. They can use different methods and materials, change the way they group the children, provide tutors and supplementary instruction, ask you to do reinforcement activities at home. They can even place a child in specific remedial programs with special teachers trained to help kids with learning problems. Many schools can provide such modifications in the instructional program without asking a child to repeat a grade.

Repeating a grade is not helpful when either the parents or the child is dead set against the idea. Under the best of circumstances, a child needs a great deal of emotional support so that he does not interpret repeating as proof of his stupidity and as a sign of failure. If this support cannot be given, for whatever reason, then the child should be promoted and other plans made for solving the academic problems.

Should you decide, in light of the above considerations, that repeating third grade would be helpful to your child, be supportive of him to ease the transition. He needs to be part of the conference when the decision is made so that he understands his own academic needs. It's imperative that he be shown both his strengths and his weaknesses so failure feelings can be minimized. Recognize and build on his strengths as much as possible. All his successes, both at home and at school, will help build his self-confidence and counteract feelings of failure.

At home, encourage him to express all of his feelings. Accept and acknowledge them; don't criticize or try to talk him out of them. He may fear that other kids will tease him and call him names which, indeed, might happen. Ask him how he'll handle the teasing. It is possible for him to learn to deal with other kids' insensitive actions. If your school has a counselor, he or she might be able to talk to your son about his feelings and generally help him adjust to repeating a grade.

7

· ·

How to Deal with Behavior Problems

You are sitting at the kitchen table with a cup of coffee, trying to calm your stunned nerves. Your son Johnny has just presented you with this note from his first grade teacher: "Please make an appointment to see me as soon as possible. Johnny's disruptive behavior is making it impossible for me to teach and for the other kids in his class to learn."

Betsy has just come home from school and, for the third time this week, is crying alone in her room. "Nobody in school likes me," she wails, "and nobody plays with me during lunch or recess."

Billy is looking you straight in the eye and shouting at the top of his lungs. "But it wasn't my fault the school window got broken, Dad. The other guys threw rocks, too. It was their idea. They told me to do it."

No parents like to be told their kid is behaving badly in school. We fear our kids' behavior problems reflect our own inadequacy as parents—it's as if, in some way, we are to blame for causing our kids to misbehave. We feel helpless because we don't have any idea how we can help our kids behave better in school when we are not there during the day to actually see what's happening and to discipline our kid.

Sooner or later, most kids experience behavior problems of one kind or another. When this happens we need to remain calm—the world is not coming to an end. Nor should we deny the problems, make excuses for our child, or shift the blame onto other kids, the teacher, the school system, television, the world situation, etc. This is the time to join forces with the school people to search for the causes and/or purposes of the unacceptable behaviors and to make specific plans to correct the situation.

Identifying the Causes and Purposes of Behavior Problems

You must deal with both the symptoms and the causes of behavior problems. When you deal with the symptoms you attempt to eliminate the specific misbehavior. When you deal with the causes and purposes you eliminate the child's under-lying need to misbehave, both now and in the future. Don't despair if it takes more time to get at the causes than to deal with the immediate misbehavior. Both steps are necessary for the well-being of your child, so stick with it.

Behavior problems in school are often a cover up for a child who is not able to cope academically, so begin by asking for an academic evaluation. A reading and math evaluation should be individually administered. Tests given to groups of children are not precise enough to uncover some hidden problems. For example, a bright child with a learning disability can often guess correctly and bluff his way through a group test. When he or she is tested individually, an experienced teacher or psychologist can usually spot his learning problems.

Sometimes behavior problems in school are a signal of stress. Perhaps there is strife in the family—parents who fight a lot, a recent separation or divorce, or even serious illness or the death of a family member. Stress could be caused by difficulties with peers—maybe a best friend has moved away or has chosen a new best friend, or perhaps other kids have excluded your child from an activity or club to which he or she aspired to be included. Even physical problems can cause stress—a poor diet, not enough sleep, insufficient exercise.

Talking and listening to your child is the best way to uncover areas of stress in his or her life. Plan specific times to be alone together, perhaps engaging in an activity that you both enjoy, and encourage him to speak. Be very careful not to cut off conversation by talking too much yourself, giving advice or lectures, judging what he or she says, or refusing to accept his or her opinions. This time is for gathering information, not planning solutions.

It will probably help if other adults talk and listen to your child. Perhaps the teacher can find a few minutes to be alone with him or her. Find out if your school has a counselor, school psychologist, or social worker—any of these professionals are trained to listen and spot difficulties. Don't overlook the services of similar professionals at local organizations such as family service agencies or mental health clinics if the problems seem severe and the school people have long waiting lists. Sometimes there's an adult outside the school to whom the child feels comfortable talking, such as a minister or rabbi, a grandparent, a scoutmaster, or a close family friend.

Look for causes of behavior problems as described above, but don't forget to consider the purposes of misbehaving in school. A child frequently receives a lot of payoffs for inappropriate behaviors.

Keeping Perspective: Your child may have 100 appropriate and positive behaviors a day, yet, if you're like most parents, two or three misbehaviors tend to overshadow these and darken your entire perception of your child. Teachers may react the same way. A child who behaves appropriately for five and three-quarter hours and causes trouble for the remaining fifteen minutes is often seen as a behavior problem. While it's necessary to follow the guidelines in this chapter to redirect misbehavior, be sure your child also gets positive recognition for all his appropriate behaviors.

It's easy to see that a child's misbehavior gains him extra attention both from his teacher and from his peers. Negative attention, perhaps, but certainly the child is noticed by all. When parents are notified of the problems in school, the child receives extra attention from mom and dad, too.

Look at all the chances to play boss a child can get by misbehaving in school. The child's message—no matter what specific misbehavior they choose—is the same. You can't make me stop, you can't make me do things your way. Power struggles between teachers and kids are probably the most frequent disruptions in classrooms today. Teachers turn prematurely gray, head for the corner bar at 3:00 P.M., or retire early from the profession when faced with too many on-going power struggles with kids day after day after day. Parents get drawn into the power struggles when teachers need more clout to overcome a child.

By misbehaving in school, a child can also get even with a parent or teacher for whatever reason seems sufficient to the child. Perhaps a parent is putting a great deal of pressure on the child to succeed or is constantly comparing the child to a more successful sibling. Maybe the teacher appears to play favorites and the kid feels left out. As one misbehaving ten-year-old said, "At least I can make them feel as miserable as I sometimes feel." Kids certainly know exactly how to do that to parents and teachers!

Children tend to hide their fear of failure. They find it easy to throw the adults off the track by misbehaving. Most adults will concentrate on the annoying behavior instead of recognizing and helping a child to overcome this fear.

Keep in mind that a combination of these causes and purposes of misbehavior may be operating in your child's case.

Planning Solutions to Behavior Problems

There is no one solution or general prescription for solving kids' behavior problems. Each child exhibits a different set of behaviors based upon a unique combination of causes and purposes. The remedy, therefore, must be tailored to the needs of the child and the specific situation. Use the following procedural guidelines to plan solutions to behavior problems.

Begin the process at a conference attended by you, the teacher, and your child. Any other people who have been involved, either in testing or talking to your child, should be included. Depending on the severity of the problem, the principal might also want to attend. If any of the adults are uncomfortable with the child, take some time to talk first without him or her. When you come, however, to the step described below on brainstorming and choosing solutions, it's very important to include the child.

First, the teacher must clearly identify, describe, and cite the frequency of the specific behaviors that are causing difficulties. The more accurate the teacher can be, the easier it will be to monitor progress. Next, information gathered as to the causes and purposes of the misbehavior can be shared.

If the underlying cause seems to be an academic problem, follow the suggestions in the last chapter for remediating academic difficulties.

For problems related to stressful situations, counseling will be helpful. Sometimes school personnel can provide short-term counseling; when they cannot, they can refer you to someone in the community who can. If the stress is caused by family problems, don't be surprised if you are also asked to go for counseling help. Some stressful situations in school can be alleviated by a change in school programs or procedures. Expect the teacher or counselor to offer such suggestions when appropriate.

See your physician if physical problems are suspected. You have the responsibility of carrying through with any recommended changes in diet, sleep or activity routines.

Behavior problems that gain the child attention, power, revenge, or avoidance of failure are a little trickier to deal with. To solve these problems, a teacher must alter his own response so that the child doesn't receive a payoff for misbehavior. A parent cannot successfully intervene in this situation because the interaction is between the teacher and the child. When parents do intervene it only reinforces the child's mistaken goal.

What you can do, however, is support the teacher in any steps he or she takes to redirect your child's misbehavior. Do not try to shield your child from any consequences that the school establishes to deal with his or her misbehavior. You can also focus on misbehavior at home that aims at a similar goal. For example, if the child is engaged in power struggles both at home and at school, any progress you make in coping at home will have a positive effect on your child's school behavior. You will be teaching your child that power struggles do not have a payoff. Refer to Appendixes 1 and 2 for resources which will help you learn to handle home situations effectively.

Your last task at the conference is to brainstorm all the

possible consequences of the child's misbehavior. It's important to include the child in this process, for most kids will cooperate more fully with plans they have helped to set up. If the child tends to play the parent against the teacher, a meeting between all concerned makes it almost impossible to continue.

After all possible solutions have been discussed the group decides which plan promises the greatest chance of success. Whatever plan is chosen should be written down to minimize the possibility of anyone misunderstanding what is going to happen.

Finish by setting up a time within the next month to get together to review the progress made toward eliminating your child's behavior problems.

Dr. Jekyll and Mr. Hyde

Q. My sixth-grade-son consistently brings home letters from two of his teachers complaining about his misbehavior. His other four teachers say he is well-adjusted and studious. Who am I to believe? Is it possible he misbehaves in some classes and not in others?

A. Any kid who is being honest will tell you that he behaves differently for different teachers. Why? Because in each classroom he must find a way to be noticed and to feel like a significant part of the class. He can choose to act cooperatively or uncooperatively, to behave appropriately or to misbehave. Unfortunately, since many teachers (parents, too) pay more attention to the misbehaving child than to the well-behaving one, it is very appealing to some kids to choose to misbehave.

A child bases his decision to behave or misbehave on three important factors: the quality of the teacher-student relationship, the strength of the classroom climate for success, and the appropriateness of the classroom structure.

Kids behave best for teachers who respond to them as individual people, not as bodies to be taught mathematics or science or English. These teachers smile a lot, talk to students in the hallways and the lunchroom, discuss matters they know are of interest to the kids. They are polite and friendly and are available to talk when the kids need an ear. They offer extra help when needed. They don't confuse being friendly with being permissive and letting the kids get away with murder in the classroom; a friendly and interested teacher can still maintain an orderly, disciplined classroom.

Kids also behave best when the classroom is programmed for success, not failure. The work is appropriately geared to the ability level of the students and daily and weekly objectives are clearly spelled out. Homework is assigned in reasonable amounts and is explained well. The grading policy is fair and consistent. Competition between students is kept to a minimum. Recognition is given to all students who work hard and participate, not just to the students who make the best grades. In such a classroom all children can experience success, not just an elite few. If a child senses he has no chance to succeed in a particular classroom, he will most likely choose to be a troublemaker to cover up his failure.

Finally, kids behave best in a classroom with a clear and consistent structure and discipline policy. Expectations and rules governing behavior are clearly spelled out. Consequences for misbehavior are established and consistently carried out. When possible, the kids have a hand in establishing and applying these consequences, through group discussions and class council meetings.

Your child has chosen different strategies to find his place in different classrooms. Talk to him about his strategies, especially with regards to the classes in which he misbehaves, and see if you can encourage him to make more appropriate choices.

Time Out!

Q. Our daughter came home from school very upset this afternoon. She said that her teacher had caught her whispering during a time when the entire class was supposed to be quiet. As punishment, our daughter had to go and sit in a special place called a "time-out area." Can you explain to me just what such an area is and why kids are punished in this way?

A. Many classrooms have a space designated as a time-out area. Sometimes this area is located behind a piano or bookcase, sometimes it is just a table or chair separated from the other children. The exact location is not important. What is important is that the time-out area removes the child from participation in classroom activities. Children go there when they are disruptive and hinder other children's learning or when they refuse to adhere to the procedures and routines that all members of the class must follow.

Generally, when a child is in a time-out area, he is not allowed to do anything except sit quietly. He does not join in the work or the fun of the classroom. Naturally your daughter didn't like being in the time-out area. It is boring and lonely to just sit. That is exactly why such time-out areas are effective. Most children prefer to cooperate and follow the classroom rules, rather than sit by themselves with nothing to do. Very often a teacher will simply say to a misbehaving child, "You have a choice of doing what you are supposed to do or sitting in the time-out area; you decide," and the misbehavior ceases.

Usually the length of time a child spends in this area is very short—five or ten minutes, perhaps. For young kids who can't tell time, a teacher will often put a kitchen timer in the area and set it for the required length of time. When the timer rings, the child can return to his regular seat. If the child continues to misbehave after returning to his seat, the teacher usually will send him to the time-out area again, only this time he will remain there for a longer period.

Time-out areas are most effective in classrooms where the children know specifically what behaviors are considered unacceptable and how long they will be expected to sit in the area when they misbehave. Classmates can be taught to ignore any child in the time-out area, thereby increasing the effectiveness of the isolation.

Your daughter views her stay in the time-out area as punishment imposed by her teacher. You might want to point out that it is instead the logical consequence of her own choice to misbehave. She could choose to follow the rules of the classroom and remain quiet when told to do so, and thus avoid the time-out area altogether.

Perish the Paddle

Q. I know from talking to other parents that sometimes the teachers or principal at our local school paddle children when they misbehave. My husband and I don't want this to happen to our son for we feel that paddling doesn't really motivate kids to behave better. Our son has gotten into trouble with his teachers a number of times over the past years, so we are afraid that sooner or later he will end up being paddled. Can a school legally paddle a child if the principal knows ahead of time that the parents object?

A. Regulations and procedures concerning corporal punishment vary from district to district. Only a small handful of states have officially banned the use of corporal punishment; a few others will honor written parental requests asking schools to refrain from using such punishment on their child. Some states that do allow paddling have established procedures that must be followed whenever a child is to receive such punishment.

From your talks with other parents, it seems apparent that corporal punishment is allowed in your district. To find out the details of the district's official policy regarding such punishment, call the superintendent of schools, a member of the Board of Education, or an officer of the local PTA. If you find that parental requests are not honored, lobby with other similarly concerned parents to change your district's policy.

You Are Not Alone Kids have peers; parents need them, too, especially parents whose kids are experiencing difficulties in school. Establish an informal discussion group of parents with problems like yours. Use the time together to provide emotional support, release frustration, exchange information, share successes and failures, and brainstorm ways to help each of your kids.

Another measure you can take to protect your child from physical punishment is to ask the school to draw up a specific plan to deal with your son's possible future misbehavior. Often teachers use paddling as a last resort because they don't know what else to do. If they are prepared with an alternative plan for handling future difficulties they will be less likely to rely on paddling to discipline your child. Follow the same procedures outlined in the introduction to this chapter for involving teachers, parents, and kids in making plans to redirect misbehavior.

Homeward Bound

Q. My third-grade daughter causes the teacher a lot of trouble in school. She fools around, doesn't pay attention, and disturbs other kids. When she is disciplined, she mouths off to the teacher and throws temper tantrums. The teacher tells me that talking to her and punishing her hasn't stopped her misbehavior. Neither has sending her to the principal's office. Now the teacher has decided that when my daughter misbehaves she will be sent home. They plan to call me at work so I can come and pick her up at school. Needless to say, I'm not crazy about the idea. I lose pay when I miss work, and my job will be in jeopardy if it happens too often. Besides, I think my daughter would love being home—she says she hates school—and will purposely misbehave just to get away. Do you think sending her home is a good solution to the problem?

A. Your daughter has obviously learned how to get a lot of negative attention. Getting sent home plays right into her plan. By misbehaving in school she gets lots of special attention from the school folks and, if sent home, she'll get some more from you. This negative attention needs to be minimized so she can learn that appropriate behavior brings more positive attention.

It is rarely productive to ask parents to provide the consequences for a child's misbehavior in school, just as it would not be effective for parents to ask teachers to provide consequences for a child's misbehaviors at home. Each area—the home and the school—must deal directly with a child's misbehavior in that environment by setting appropriate rules and limits and by providing immediate consequences when these are disobeyed.

As an alternative to sending kids home, many schools have established an in-school suspension policy. A room is designated for such use, and a teacher, counselor, aide, or combination of these supervises this room. A benefit of in-school suspensions is that it allows a cooling-off separation for both the teacher and the student when they are upset with each other. What kids do during in-school suspension varies from school to school. In some places, the kids are required just to sit. They are not allowed to read, do classwork, or any other activity. It is expected that they will get bored and lonely and frustrated by having nothing to do and will behave appropriately when allowed to return to the classroom. Other schools allow or require the kids to work quietly, believing that separation from their classmates will be enough of an incentive for the child to behave appropriately afterward.

A different consequence for misbehavior is used by the Pinellas County Schools in Florida. Administrators require kids who have misbehaved to attend school on Saturday morning. The program on Saturday includes classes designed to improve kids' study habits, communication skills, and interpersonal relationships. Administrators, parents, and students in the district feel the benefits gained from the Saturday school program outweigh the costs involved.

If your school does not have similar alternatives for children who misbehave, talk to the administrators and PTA about setting one up.

Should you have to bring her home while other plans are being made, don't make the time particularly pleasant. No extra attention. No television. No activities with mom or dad. Staying quietly in her room during the hours she would be in school is appropriate.

Later in the day invite her to talk about her feelings and her problems. Listen and be supportive. Remember, it's her problem. Though we want to solve our kids' problems to make life easier for them, it's not possible. Encourage her to think of ways to get along better in school. State your expectation that she'll be able to behave in school when she chooses to.

Enjoy a pleasant evening together. Kids (and parents) don't have to suffer afterwards for a consequence to be effective.

Suspended from School

Q. Last Wednesday my son came home with a letter from the school principal telling me that he was being suspended from school for three days because he had left the school playground without permission for the third time this month. I was shocked! First, because I didn't know he had been in trouble before—the school had not bothered to notify me. Second, I don't think suspension is a very effective solution. My son isn't fond of going to school anyway, so he liked the idea of staying home for three days. Does the school have the legal right to suspend a kid just like that?

A. There are very specific due process procedures regarding school suspensions. These rulings were established by the U.S. Supreme Court case known as *Goss v. Lopez,* 1975. Before a student can be suspended from school, notice must be given, either orally or in writing, to the student and the parent. This notice must state clearly the charges against the student and the evidence that the school has substantiating these charges. The student has a right to tell his or her side of the story before the final decision is reached.

When the above procedures are followed schools do have a right to suspend students who break school rules, as a disciplinary measure. Ideally, all school rules should be written down so that parents and children are aware of what the rules are. If your school doesn't have the rules written down, suggest through the school PTA that such a list be established.

A parent should be notified immediately when a serious infraction of a school rule occurs, regardless of whether any action is taken at that point.

There are often more effective disciplinary actions than suspension, especially for elementary school students. If your child gets in trouble again in the future, make an appointment to meet with your child's teacher and the school principal at once. See if together you can come up with other ideas for disciplining your son. It's generally very helpful for your son to participate in the conference. It's important for him to see that breaking rules is a serious business, that his parents are very concerned, and that unpleasant consequences will occur.

If the school does decide to suspend your child again, don't make the days at home pleasant for him. He should stay in the house during the hours school is in session, and not be allowed to wander about town. He should have assignments to complete during regular school hours. Don't entertain him.

Let him discover how boring it is to be at home while all his friends are in school. Many kids brag about how much they'd rather be home but when they experience a few boring days alone they quickly realize that the real "action" is in school.

Help for the Hyperactive

Q. My son just can't stop moving and sit still; not at home and not at school. His teacher suggests medication. If I can find other ways to help him, I'd prefer not to use drugs. Where should I begin?

A. Begin with a complete professional evaluation of his problem. See your pediatrician for a physical and talk over the problem. The doctor should be able to recommend a neurologist and a psychologist to evaluate your son. Ideally, the three doctors will communicate with each other, share their findings, come up with a diagnosis and recommend a course of action. Some cities have clinics geared to diagnosing such problems, where all the testing can be done in one place. To find out if there's such a clinic near your home, ask your pediatrician, the social worker or psychologist assigned to your child's school, or write to the Association for Children with Learning Disabilities, 4156 Library Road, Pittsburgh, PA 15234.

Ask your pediatrician if adjusting your son's diet will help. Some children apparently are allergic to specific foods or chemicals which trigger hyperactivity. Many parents report success with what's known as the Feingold diet, although research has yet to prove the efficacy of such an approach. If your pediatrician doesn't test for allergies, he may be able to recommend someone who can.

Provide plenty of opportunity for your son to dispel some of his excess energy. A mat for tumbling and a punching bag are a good start. If either parent likes to run, teach your son to jog along. Many kids who run before school have a much easier time sitting still during class. Some schools have even organized before-school running programs for just this reason.

Structure the home environment. He needs consistent rules and routines. Events like mealtime, bedtime, and bathtime should occur at the same time every day. Be firm and consistent in adhering to schedules. Don't let his apparent inability to sit still become an excuse for not conforming to the same rules and routines as the rest of the family. Kids often use small disabilities to put the rest of the family in their service, to get special attention, and to get out of doing things they don't want to do. Don't let this happen.

Keep his environment as simple as possible. Rotate his toys so there are not too many out at one time. Calm music, soft lights, and subdued colors may have a quieting effect. Avoid rousing activities before mealtime and bedtime.

If your child's evaluation indicates that medication would be useful, be sure that it is monitored very carefully. You and his teacher should keep written records describing your son's behavior, particularly any changes noticed. When improvement occurs, the medication may be able to be gradually decreased and withdrawn.

Last of all, plan time for yourself away from your son, doing activities you like. Pamper yourself—get a haircut, play bridge, go for a walk. Raising kids who can't sit still is an extremely difficult task. A little rest and relaxation for the parent, away from home, will help you cope with the other times.

Life as a Loner

Q. I have a daughter who is a loner, both at home and at school. Teachers have often told me that she has few friends at school, sits by herself in the cafeteria, and doesn't like to go out on the playground at lunch time. At home she'd much rather read or watch TV than go outside and play with the neighborhood kids. Should I just accept the fact that she's a loner and leave her alone, or is there something I can do to help her become more outgoing?

A. Accept the fact that some children naturally seem to be more outgoing than others. Some like to hang around with a crowd, others prefer to stick with one or two close friends. Don't put constant pressure on your daughter to change—the more you do, the more she'll resist your efforts. Be careful not to use the label "loner" and "shy" in her presence, for that will only reinforce the behaviors you would like to change.

You can, however, help her form some friendships without using pressure. Invite another family with a daughter her age to share activities with your family. Perhaps a joint supper or a movie or an evening of Monopoly would be fun. Make your yard an inviting place for neighborhood children to come to play. Some children feel OK about playing with others as long as they are close to home. Encourage her to join any activity groups in which she shows interest, particularly if the activity is a non-competitive one. Swimming, gymnastics, ballet, scouts, and library book clubs are all possibilities. Friendships can grow from shared interests and activities.

The school is in an even better position to help your child form friendships. Visit her school and talk with all of her teachers. The object of your visit is to make the teachers more aware of who your child is, especially her strengths, special interests, and any unusual and exciting experiences she has had. Teachers are so busy that frequently they don't take the time to look behind the quiet exterior of a shy child. When they know your child better, teachers can devise ways to help foster friendships. One way might be to organize a special interest group that studies a subject and makes a presentation to the class. Another might be to pair your daughter with another child who needs extra help in a subject that your daughter knows well. Some schools organize special activity groups at lunch time to mix kids who are usually alone with others who are outgoing.

Teach Open Communication Early   Teach kids to use speech and language as a tool to communicate openly. Communicating openly means expressing your feelings, needs, and dreams. It means saying what's on your mind. Kids who communicate openly talk about the world within themselves, as well as the outside world. Children who seem "shy" or "non-talkative" may simply not have learned this important communication skill.

The skill of open communication broadens a kid's world and his or her ability to make close contact with others. Help your kids develop this skill by talking with them every day. Gently ask about their feelings and dreams. Talk about your own inner life, too. By expressing your feelings, you model the skill for your kids to copy.

The point is that it's not enough for the school just to report to you that your daughter is a loner. Specific plans need to be made to encourage her to join in more with the other children. You can help by providing the information they need to get to know your daughter as a complete person, not just a face in the crowd.

Lunchroom Woes

Q.   Today the school principal called to tell me I must come to take my thirteen-year-old son out to lunch for the next two weeks. Because of bad behavior, he is being banned from the school lunchroom. While I understand that a principal cannot allow certain behaviors, this seems like the wrong way to change them. My son would love going out with me far more than eating in the school cafeteria. Won't this really reward him for the misbehavior and encourage it to continue?

A. Few people recall their experiences in school lunchrooms with much pleasure. The noise and confusion of hundreds of kids eating at once, chattering and letting off steam after sitting quietly in class all morning, can be nerve-racking. And who has ever raved about the quality and taste of school cafeteria food? If the payoff for misbehavior in the lunchroom becomes a trip home or to McDonalds' with Mom or Dad, what kid isn't smart enough to learn to misbehave to get such privileges?

Your principal is right, however, in knowing that he needs to take effective action. Words will not influence your son to change his behavior. Most likely your son has been asked repeatedly to stop misbehaving and has ignored reminders, warnings, and threats. Actions, not words, will teach him the connection between his behavior and its consequences.

An effective action for the principal to take is to give your son a choice. He can behave and continue to eat in the lunchroom or he can decide to misbehave, in which case he may not enter the lunchroom for a day. The principal needs to clarify which specific behaviors are acceptable and which are not.

Where will your son go while the others are eating if he is barred from the lunchroom and his parents don't take him out? The playground, if a supervisor is available during the entire lunch period? The principal's office? A detention room? Different schools have different places where a misbehaving child may go.

He will not starve if barred from the cafeteria. No doubt he's smart enough to figure out that he'll have to brown-bag a sandwich for lunch. Making the lunch is his job, not yours. Stay out of his problem with the school and let him experience the consequences for his misbehavior. He owns the problem.

When faced with the unpleasant consequences of his own misbehavior, including separation from his friends and having to prepare his own lunch or go hungry, he may decide rather quickly to change his lunchroom behaviors.

Making Music Miserable

Q. I just received a note from my daughter's music teacher. It seems my daughter is causing trouble because she refuses to sing with the other children. The teacher asks that I talk with my daughter to see if I can get her to cooperate better in class. Do you suppose if I ground her from visiting friends or ban TV for a while that she will learn to cooperate with her music teacher?

A. I doubt it. It sounds as though the teacher and your daughter are caught up in a classic power struggle. When they sense the child is winning, teachers frequently request a parent's help in power situations. I'm sure the teacher hopes that you will add your power to his or hers in the hope of forcing your daughter to sing.

I wonder how teachers would feel if a parent asked for help when engaged in a home power struggle with a kid. Suppose a parent whose child refused to make his bed called the teacher and asked him to have a talk with the child about the necessity of making his bed each day. Maybe the teacher could keep the child after school for a week as punishment for not making his bed at home!

The adult directly involved in a power struggle with a child—the parent or the teacher—is in the best position to solve the problem.

The teacher wants your help in influencing your daughter to cooperate. That's fine. When parents and teachers support each other it's the child who benefits. The type of support you give, however, makes a vast difference. Becoming another player in a power struggle is not helpful; becoming a listener and a problem solver is.

It is appropriate for you to talk to your daughter about her thoughts and feelings concerning the music class problem. Talk in a calm, non-critical and non-judgmental way. The purpose of the talk is not to tell her she is wrong or behaving badly in school; the object is to get out her feelings and find what it is about the music class that influences her to decide not to be cooperative. Then ask her what she thinks she can do to solve her problem. No one can force her to sing. Any suggestions she comes up with have a much better chance of working than any punishment you impose.

Once you know her thoughts and feelings, and she has thought of possible ways to solve the problem, a conference between the teacher, your daughter, and you is called for. The purpose of the conference is to look at the problem, brainstorm possible solutions, and come up with a plan acceptable to all three of you. With you and her teacher present, your daughter cannot play "divide and conquer" and pit the school against the home.

Support such requests from teachers for help—not by imposing arbitrary consequences at home, but by becoming a partner in seeking reasonable in-school solutions.

No Excuses, Please

Q. The principal of my son's school called this afternoon to tell me that my son was part of a group of four boys who broke some windows after school. He wants to meet with all the kids' parents tomorrow to discuss the situation. Billy's in fourth grade and has never been in trouble in school before. He says it was the other kids' idea, that his friends made him do it, and he promises never to do anything like this again. Since it's his first offense, should we suggest that the school overlook it and give him another chance to prove himself?

A. Sooner or later, most kids find themselves in a tough spot, from which they learn difficult lessons about personal responsibility, peer pressure, and the consequences of their behavior. Your son is in just such a position right now. It's crucial to handle the situation so that it becomes an effective lesson he'll long remember.

To do this, concentrate only on his behavior—in this case, the broken window. Don't make any negative statements about him as a person. Don't feel sorry for him. Don't overreact by predicting a terrible future. He is not a bad kid with a ticket straight to reform school just because he broke a window. His behavior, however, is unacceptable and needs to be corrected. Treat this as a single mistake, but make sure to voice the expectation that it won't ever happen again.

Don't Predict the Future The fact that your child is experiencing behavior problems in school today does not guarantee future difficulties and an unsuccessful life. Many parents overreact to school problems by predicting a disastrous future for their children. In reality, with time, effort, and cooperation between home and school, many of today's problems can be overcome without leaving any lasting marks on your child.

Do not accept his excuse that others made him do it. No matter what the surrounding circumstances, his decision to throw the rock was his alone. He cannot escape personal responsibility for his decision. Yes, peer pressure is strong. But some kids resist the negative influences. Your son can, too. The choice of going along with the crowd or saying no belongs to him.

He must be allowed to experience the consequences of breaking a window. The most logical consequence is that he will assume responsibility for paying all or part of the replacement cost. He can contribute money from a savings account if he has one, or from his allowance. What he can't afford to pay, he can work for by performing services for the school. Kids can sweep, wash walls and windows, empty trash, and so on. What they do isn't as important as the fact that they are doing it.

Should the school not wish to supervise kids working, you may have to pay part of the replacement costs yourself and have your son work at home to earn his share.

Do not excuse him from the consequences of his misbehavior on the grounds that it was his first offense. It's these consequences that will most strongly influence him not to repeat this behavior in the future.

Bully Beats Up Others

Q. The teacher says my eight-year-old daughter picks on other kids. She grabs things away, pinches, and calls names in the classroom. On the playground during recess she often kicks and fights. She tells me that she doesn't like the other kids and that they don't like her. I see similar problems after school with the kids in the neighborhood. What should we be doing to help my daughter at home and at school?

A. Begin by teaching her the language of cooperative play. She needs to know how to ask for something she wants if another child is using it. Teach her to say "I want to play with _____. Will you give it to me when you are finished with it?" Conversely, when another child covets something with which she is playing, teach her to be assertive and say, "I am using this now. You may have it when I am through."

She also needs to know how to ask to join another child or group of children who are playing: "May I play with you?" "Would you like to play with me?" It's easy for adults to take this language for granted and assume that all kids know the words. They don't. In fact, kids need to learn the same assertive skills that many adults must learn. They need to learn how to state their feelings and their needs directly and calmly. Kids with good assertiveness skills have much less need for aggressive behavior.

Ideally, teachers should teach these language skills to all children, beginning in nursery school. The lessons need to be repeated many times over, with puppets, with stories, with kids role-playing the situations over and over again. Should the teacher be too busy to include these lessons, or feel that all the rest of the class already has the skills, perhaps a school counselor could do the teaching instead. Counselors can bring together kids from different classes experiencing similar difficulties and work just with them.

All adults who work with your daughter need to give her special recognition and attention when she cooperates with other kids, rather than when she bullies them. The pattern of getting attention for inappropriate behavior needs to be reversed. Ignore situations when she acts like a bully but no one else is in danger of being hurt. When there is that danger, she must be separated from others for a time-out period. See page 113 for using time-outs effectively. This can be done at home, too.

She also needs strategies for expressing and releasing her angry and hostile feelings. Hitting a pillow, tossing beanbags, pounding clay, punching a punching bag, banging with a foam bat are all appropriate ways. She most likely needs a place to do this both at home and at school.

Many schools are flexible enough to plan positive experiences for kids who have difficulties with their peers. School counselors can offer group counseling sessions. Teachers can arrange peer tutoring sessions, where one kid teaches a skill he has mastered to another, often younger, child. Small groups of kids can be given the responsibility of performing some necessary school service, such as helping with audio-visual equipment or monitoring street crossings. All such experiences will help your daughter form friendships and find a significant place to belong through positive rather than negative behavior.

You can promote friendships by encouraging her to invite one child at a time home to play. Structure the time so that you do some activities with them, but leave them plenty of time on their own.

Pay particular attention to the three R's of raising kids—rules, routines, and responsibilities—particularly if your daughter is using bullying tactics at home to get her own way. Learn the three R's in a parenting course such as STEP (Systematic Training for Effective Parenting) or Active Parenting or read the books listed in Appendix 1.

The Sun Will Come Out Tomorrow Let each day be a new day. Expect that yesterday's problems will not be repeated. Don't lock your child into future behavior problems by constant reminders of past transgressions. Be prepared to take corrective action should your child misbehave, but at the same time express your confidence that he will choose to behave appropriately instead.

8

• •

How to Seek
Services from the
School Specialists

"Please sign this permission slip so Mrs. Williams, our school social worker, can see your daughter," says the note Suzie just brought home from school. School social worker? You didn't know such a person exists. What does she do? Why does she want to see Suzie? Is your child in some kind of trouble?

Kevin has been rubbing his eyes a lot lately when he reads or watches TV. Is he just tired or could he have an eyesight problem? Should you take him to an eye doctor? Could the school nurse take a look at him and tell you what to do next?

Mrs. Kelly, Johnny's teacher, has been sick a lot lately. Johnny talks a lot about the different teachers who have been substituting for her. Who are these substitute teachers and how qualified are they to take over for the regular classroom teacher?

Most parents' contact with the school staff is limited to their kids' classroom teachers. Teachers send home the newsletters and report cards. They conduct the open-house sessions and parent conferences. The adult mentioned most frequently when kids talk about what's happening in school is the classroom teacher. Yet the teacher is only one member of a large team of professionals assembled to help you and your kids. Other team members may include the principal, counselor, psychologist, social worker, nurse, reading specialist, special education teacher, speech and language therapist, and librarian. Not every school employs all of these specialists. Once schools have fulfilled federal and state mandates, they are free to set priorities and hire specialists accordingly.

The function of each of these team members is to help your kids succeed in school by providing a variety of specialized services for you and your kids, all at no direct expense to you! You have already learned about the remedial services provided by reading specialists and special education teachers in Chapter five. This chapter will help you understand who the rest of these people are, what they can do for your kids, and how to make sure your kids get their services when needed.

Most of these school people can provide direct diagnostic and remedial services to kids. Some will provide direct services to parents as well. They are available for short-term consultations when you need specific advice concerning your kids and for referrals to other community agencies when long-term services are needed.

The classroom teacher usually initiates the process whereby a child receives special services from one or more of these school people. When the teacher suspects a problem, he or she will usually talk to the person who specializes in that particular problem area. For example, if a teacher suspects a child has a hearing problem, the nurse and/or speech therapist will be consulted. Before the specialist sees your child you will most likely be asked for written permission.

As a parent, you can also initiate the process and request special help. Begin by talking to the teacher, by phone or in person, describing the problem you suspect and asking for an appointment with the appropriate specialist. Or you can call the specialist directly and ask for a brief meeting in which you present the suspected problem and ask for help.

Teacher of the Month Award   Join with other parents to give special recognition to the outstanding teachers in your school. Honor one teacher each month with a special award: a framed certificate of recognition, a cake, honorable mention in a school newsletter, or even a dinner for two at a local restaurant. Most teachers work very long hours for relatively poor pay and rarely receive recognition or thanks for their efforts. Watch teacher morale in your kids' school soar when they know parents care enough to notice what they do.

Be aware there are often long waiting lists for services from school people who are in short supply and high demand, like school psychologists. There are also local, state, and federal guidelines that specify who qualifies for which services and who does not. You may feel that your child needs remedial reading services, for example, but unless his test scores fall into a prescribed range that meets these guidelines, such services will not be provided.

When you wish your child to receive specialized services that the school can't provide, ask the school people to refer you to other professionals or agencies in the community who can supply the service. Also ask them to serve as a liaison between whatever outside service you choose and the school to see that both programs are coordinated to meet the needs of your child.

Be a smart parent—get to know these people and the services they provide. Ask for their help when you need it.

Need a Nurse?

Q. We moved to a new school district this year. In our last school if a child felt ill during the school day the school nurse saw the child and decided whether or not the child should be sent home. In this school the nurse refuses to try to see what the illness is. She says her job is mainly to keep immunization records, treat cuts and bruises, and keep track of medications that doctors prescribe for some kids during the day, not to diagnose illness. I'm confused by these differences in approach and want to know what I can expect from the school nurse.

A. Medical services provided for children by the schools vary because of school policy and the nurse's expertise. School nurses can be aides or paraprofessionals with a minimum of special training or nurse-teachers who have earned both nursing and teaching degrees. The more training and experience a school nurse has acquired, the more services he or she can offer to kids and parents.

At the very least, the school nurse treats minor cuts and bruises and refers serious accidents or illnesses to the proper medical practitioners. She keeps the school health records, particularly immunization data. She dispenses medication during the day that has been prescribed by a physician and requested—usually in writing—by parents. When a parent is new to a community, the school nurse can serve as an information source for finding appropriate medical care for the family.

The school nurse also plays an important role in a child's readjustment to school after a serious illness or hospitalization.

She links the child's doctor and the school. It is the nurse who keeps all of the school personnel informed about the nature and management of a child's medical needs and sees that the doctor's recommendations for program adjustment, especially in the area of physical activity, are followed. It is the nurse who reports back to the doctor when any physical symptoms or radical behavior changes occur, especially if there's a suspected reaction to medication. This information helps the doctor to make future decisions concerning your child.

Nurses with more training provide hearing and vision screening services for kids. Referrals for further diagnostic work and treatment are made for any child suspected of having such difficulties.

In addition to the above duties, nurse-teachers are part of the diagnostic team that determines the causes of a child's school problems. Nurses can review past and current medical history and can observe a child during the school day for symptoms that might point to underlying medical difficulties. They can serve as a liaison between any physicians who have seen the child and the school staff. When a child who has a chronic illness returns to school after hospitalization or a severe illness, the nurse–teacher monitors school adjustment and reports back to the physician as necessary.

Most nurse-teachers are also qualified to conduct first aid classes for kids and to teach family life and sex education in the classroom.

Is it worth the extra cost to hire a nurse-teacher instead of an aide? Considering the services only a trained nurse-teacher can provide, the answer is probably yes. But each district must set its own priorities within limited resources.

Count on the Counselor

Q. I can't understand why our school district wants to hire guidance counselors for the elementary schools. Because I have two older kids, I know that counselors in the junior and senior high schools are responsible for helping with the kids' class schedules and college applications and career decisions. But since these services are not needed for younger kids, who spend most of their day with the same teacher, why spend the money?

A. It's unfortunate that so many parents associate school counselors mainly with class schedules and college applications. In reality these highly trained and specialized professionals can provide many other important services for kids. This is especially important for young children, still at the formative stage where patterns of behavior and interactions in school have not been firmly established. The earlier a child experiencing difficulties receives help, the greater the chances for success.

Counselors are trained to provide a variety of services to kids, parents, and teachers. They help kids with personal identity problems. Some kids need to raise their self-esteem and self-confidence. Others need to learn to accept their individual strengths, weaknesses, and differences. Still others need to explore and perhaps change their attitudes toward their family, their school, and/or their community.

Counselors can also help kids with relationships. Some kids have behaviors that hinder friendships, such as shyness or aggression. Others have difficulty relating to teachers. They may be disruptive because they seek too much attention, engage the teacher in power struggles, or desire revenge. Some kids experience difficulties at home because of a change in family structure due to death, separation, divorce, or remarriage.

Counselors provide a variety of services for these children. They may counsel a child individually for a short period of time, referring those kids who need long-term individual counseling to community agencies. They may counsel a small group of kids experiencing similar difficulties. Or they may lead guidance activities in an entire classroom of children.

Services to parents can also be individual or group. When a counselor is involved with a child he can usually provide parents with insights regarding their child's behavior and academic, social, and emotional development. He can suggest how the parents can best help the child at home. In groups, many counselors provide parent-training workshops in various skills, such as discipline or communication skills.

Counselors also serve as consultants to teachers. They provide information about guidance activities that teachers can do with the whole class. They suggest discipline techniques to teachers who need such ideas. They keep kids' test records on file and make these available to teachers as needed.

When problems arise in the lunchroom, in the hall, or on the playground, counselors become instrumental in establishing school policies and procedures for dealing with these difficulties.

Finally, counselors, because of their training in communication and problem-solving skills, often serve as facilitators during conferences to solve conflicts between kids or between parents and their children's teachers.

Counselors in the elementary schools are not usually mandated by the state. However, more and more districts are discovering the benefits such specialists bring to a school staff and are making the decision to hire counselors anyway. Support your district in this effort. Use the counselor's services when you or your kids have a need that they are trained to help.

Seek Out the Psychologist

Q. My daughter doesn't behave well in school. The school psychologist told my wife and me that she has emotional problems and needs counseling. I agree she needs help because we have problems with her at home, too. But I don't understand why the school psychologist doesn't counsel our daughter herself instead of giving us a list of other psychologists to call. She could save us a lot of money and inconvenience since my wife and I both work. Should we insist the school provide such help?

A. Few public schools provide intensive counseling for psychological or behavioral problems; the time and cost involved is beyond what most schools can afford. Consider yourself lucky that a school psychologist was available to evaluate your daughter's problems and to make a recommendation and referral. Even those services are beyond the means of some schools.

School psychologists assess children's academic potential and abilities and evaluate social and emotional problems. The results of these tests are used to determine if children qualify for special services or special class placements under the laws that govern the education of handicapped kids. School psychologists also serve as consultants to classroom teachers and help them plan programs and procedures for children experiencing difficulties in school. One school psychologist often serves the children and teachers of more than one school. It's not unusual to find that one school psychologist is responsible for 2500 or 3000 students. Quite a staggering case load!

Thus, when your school psychologist identified problems she thought would require many weeks or months of therapeutic counseling for your daughter, she suggested outside agencies better suited to the task than the school. Mental health or family service centers are staffed with counseling psychologists and/or social workers especially trained in individual and family therapy and who are qualified to help your daughter overcome her problems. You can expect the school psychologist, however, to keep in touch with your daughter's counselor in order to coordinate any suggestions the counselor makes to the school.

Seeking help outside the school needn't bankrupt you, either. Most community agencies use a sliding scale that gears fees to your income.

Don't be surprised if you and your wife are asked to participate in some or all of the counseling sessions. Many psychologists consider counseling the entire family much more effective than just treating the one person who exhibits problems.

Forget Their Failures Do your children a favor and forget their failures. Forever. In hopes of motivating their children to succeed, parents often dwell on previous mistakes, accidents, poor grades, or irresponsible behaviors. This approach usually backfires. Reminders of past failures only pave the way for future failures.

Work with the School Social Worker

Q. Our school has hired a part-time social worker. We're surprised that the school has added new personnel since they keep telling parents that programs have to be cut because money is so tight. What good can a social worker do in a school setting?

A. A social worker is a valuable member of any school staff. Lucky is the district that finds the money to employ one, even if it's only a part-time position. A social worker has valuable skills to help the child who experiences difficulties in school. While other school personnel do educational and psychological testing to pinpoint specific difficulties a child might experience, the social worker concentrates on fostering home-school cooperation to solve a child's problems.

There are three types of problems for which a child is likely to be referred to the social worker. One is a problem with attitude toward school. A child with a poor attitude achieves little and lacks the motivation and interest to improve. A social-emotional difficulty is the second type of problem commonly referred to social workers. A child might have trouble maintaining friendships because he is too aggressive or too shy. Or he might be so disruptive in class that the teacher has difficulty teaching. Perhaps he spends most of his time daydreaming, rarely joining group activities. A third type of problem referred to social workers is an attendance problem. A child might skip school outright, or constantly arrive late, or consistently feign illness to avoid going to school at all.

Only Time Every child of every age needs a good dose of "only time" a few times a week. This is time a parent spends talking only to that child, and only about subjects related to that child. It provides a great opportunity to talk to your child about his or her dreams and accomplishments, or worries, uncertainties, and setbacks. Set up the environment so nobody and nothing else can interrupt this time. These often are the moments when a parent has the greatest influence on a child. These are the moments that the child will remember and treasure in the future.

Once a child has been referred to the social worker, he begins to gather information that clarifies the problem. To do this, he gets involved in all areas of the child's life. The social worker talks to the child's teachers and observes the child in the classroom, on the playground, perhaps even on the school bus. He visits the parents at home where he asks questions about the child's home environment. Candid answers to these questions are essential for the social worker, who must understand the child's world and how the child perceives his world. Most likely the social worker will also have a few sessions talking with the child himself.

The job of the social worker doesn't stop here, however. Occasionally he will become involved with your child for short-term counseling, or perhaps for periodic counseling sessions over a few months to assess your child's progress. If the social worker perceives a need for long-term counseling, either for the child or for the parents, he will refer you to an outside agency. If it is necessary for any other type of community agency to become involved with the child or the family, the social worker often makes the initial referral and is the liaison between the home, the school, and the agency.

The social worker is also a resource for parents, especially in elementary schools that do not have counselors. If there is a major change in the family, either an impending separation or divorce, a serious illness, or a severe change in economic status, a parent may want advice about how to handle the situation with his or her children. The school social worker is prepared to give such advice and to make referrals to other community agencies if more intensive help is necessary.

Occasionally a school social worker will get involved with a family at the request of a community agency such as social services or the courts. This happens when personnel in these agencies, who are involved with a particular child or family, want to know more about what is happening with this child at school or to suggest specific changes in the school program that they feel will benefit the child.

The differences in roles between the social worker, counselor, and psychologist can be confusing; all these professionals are qualified to counsel kids and parents. Psychologists focus mainly on testing, counselors on in-school services, and social workers on fostering home-school and sometimes home-school-community agency cooperation. Don't hesitate to call on any of them when you want assistance for your child. Should you contact the incorrect person for the help you are seeking, that person will undoubtedly steer you to the appropriate professional.

Speak to the Speech Teacher

Q. My seven-year-old son stutters and mispronounces many words. When he was younger we thought he'd outgrow these problems. Now we're beginning to worry, especially because his stuttering embarasses him, and other kids mimic his mistakes. Is there a special teacher in the school who should be helping him with these difficulties?

A. Children with either speech, hearing, or language difficulties should be evaluated by a certified speech and language therapist early in their school career. These professionals determine the extent of the problem and provide remedial services for the children who qualify based on the evaluation results. They also make referrals to other community resources when appropriate.

Only extremely large schools have speech and language therapists on their full-time staff—most schools have to share this professional with at least one or two other schools. Small schools don't have enough children requiring services to fill the therapist's time. Many school districts, facing tight budgets, economize by having schools share services.

Request an evaluation for your son. Talk to the classroom teacher first because he or she can give you some idea how your child's problems compare to other kids the same age. Then ask the teacher to put in the request for services from the speech and language therapist. Once the testing has been done, you are entitled to conference with the therapist, have the results of the evaluation explained to you, and participate in making a remediation plan. Be sure to ask the therapist for hints on how you should handle the speech problems at home.

Love That Librarian

Q. My youngest daughter, Betsy, doesn't show much interest in reading. She does her reading homework, but rarely picks up a book just for the fun ot it. It's not that she can't read, it's just that she won't. Should I ignore the problem or is there something else I could be doing?

A. Your best ally in fostering a love of books is the school librarian. School librarians can match books to kids. They can find fiction or nonfiction that sparks a child's interest. They know which books a third-grader could probably read with little difficulty and which ones require greater reading skills. They can suggest stories for kids with reading problems that will capture interest without being too difficult to read. They are able to steer kids to special interest children's magazines and sometimes even to audio tapes and records. In many schools librarians offer creative literature programs designed to entice youngsters into a love of reading.

School librarians are excellent resources for parents, too. Need suggestions for books to read aloud? For books to buy your kids for birthday presents? On educational magazines that might interest your kids? Perhaps there's a special situation in your family—a recent death of a grandparent, a serious illness, a child with a handicap, or an impending divorce—and you'd like books that will help your kids better understand the situation and themselves. Many school libraries even have a "Parent Resource Shelf" where you can find the latest advice books on raising children.

The advantage of the school librarian is that he or she knows the school curriculum and is likely to have frequent informal interaction with your child. Make an appointment to visit the librarian. Explain your daughter's situation. Discuss your daughter's special interests and hobbies; knowing these will help the librarian find books that might appeal to her. Ask him or her to make a special effort to get to know your child and to invite her to use the library, check out books, and to take part in any creative literature programs the school offers. A friendly librarian who says to a child on the playground, "I have a new book and I'm saving it just for you because I think you'll really enjoy it," has a terrific chance of influencing a child's reading habits.

Principals Pave the Path

Q. I'm on a committee to choose a new principal for the school my daughter attends. What do you think the committee should look for in a principal?

A. Most parents remember the principal as the person to whom the "bad" kids were sent to be disciplined. The principal gave lectures, called parents, and suspended or even paddled kids when appropriate.

An effective principal is much more than the chief disciplinarian in a school. Think of your school as an organization. The leader of any organization is the key to how smoothly the organization runs and to how well the goals of the organization are articulated and achieved. The principal you seek will head the school organization and thus will have ultimate responsibility for the daily functioning of the school and for the education of the students.

The day-to-day operation of the school, its maintenance, its budget, its records—all are a principal's responsibility. He or she must also make sure that the school adheres to local, state, and federal guidelines, and must produce the required paperwork as proof. Many of these duties can be delegated to others, though the principal retains the final responsibility. The buck stops in the principal's office, so you want to find a person with effective management skills who can run the school smoothly and efficiently.

More important than this administrative role is the role of educational leader. Good schools cannot exist in a vacuum. A school must have a leader who clearly sets the school climate by articulating goals and expectations, and who establishes the curriculum and instructional procedures to be used in achieving the stated goals.

To be an effective educational leader, the principal must be prepared to leave the office for the majority of the day in order to be in the classrooms, so that he is fully aware of what is taking place. He must be able to effectively support and evaluate the teaching staff by observing, giving specific feedback, making appropriate suggestions for improvement, and making sure that the suggestions are carried out. When teachers are absent, the principal must choose and supervise the substitute teachers.

He must also have the knowledge and intuition to spot problems as they appear. Are the school's achievement scores down? Are there children for whom the school program doesn't seem to be effective? Are there children who require special programs mandated by the federal government? Are the discipline, absentee, or drop-out problems on the increase? The principal must have both the initiative and the skills to find solutions to these problems.

The principal also must have the desire and skill to work with the parents in the community and to support parental involvement in the school. When individuals or groups of parents seek to change some school policy or portion of the curriculum, the principal must be available to listen and take appropriate action. He or she must have good negotiating and peacemaking skills, so that differing factions of the community can be brought into relative harmony. Peacemaking skills are often needed within the school building, too. It is the principal who must facilitate disputes among staff members and even among children who fight.

Lastly, look for someone with the health and stamina to put in the long hours necessary to accomplish all of the above tasks.

9

● ●

How to Make Sense of School Programs and Policies

Your five-year-old son is in nursery school again this year because his birthday falls in December, after the cutoff date for entering kindergarten. Yet your niece, who lives in another state and who is two weeks younger than your son, is in kindergarten because January 1 is the cutoff entrance date in that state.

Your daughters receive art instruction twice a week from a special teacher trained in art education. They bring home all kinds of exciting projects—clay bowls, large collages, tie-dyed T-shirts, mosaics made from seeds. While visiting a friend who lives just twenty miles away, in a different school district, you discover that his children never attend art classes. Their art education is limited to occasional pictures drawn during the

145

day in their regular classrooms after their academic work is completed.

A friend of yours lives within walking distance, but her kids attend a different school in the same district because the school boundary lines happen to fall between your houses. Your six-year-old sons like to play together while you drink coffee and chat. The other day you were comparing the kids' school books and found that their readers were totally different. One boy had a book with attractive colorful pictures and just a few words on each page. The other's reader had no pictures at all and consisted of lots of words that all seemed alike such as *cat, sat,* and *rat.* It seemed strange that kids in the same school district didn't use the same textbooks.

No uniform code of educational policies and practices exists in this country. There are a few federal mandates, such as providing services to children with handicapping conditions, that all schools must follow. Outside of these, the individual states set their own rules and regulations, which can differ greatly from state to state. Once state and federal guidelines have been met, local school districts are then free to establish programs and policies based on their own needs and priorities.

As federal funds for education dry up and citizens veto school budgets, cutbacks on programs and services not mandated by the state or federal government are often the first economy move a district makes. An entire program might be cut out altogether. Or the level of services may be reduced so that one special services teacher might have to split time between two or even three schools. Two factors influence which programs and services are cut: community interest and pressure to support a particular program and the organized strength of the district's special teachers.

As a parent, you can influence the decisions that control the policies and programs in the schools your kids attend, especially if you join forces with other parents who wish to have a similar impact. Your greatest ally is a strong parents' organization. The PTA today, on all levels—local, district, state, and national—is very active in fostering parent awareness of policies and programs and in lobbying for changes. The National Committee on Citizens in Education also serves as a clearinghouse for parents wishing more information on any given issue and as a resource for parents searching for strategies to initiate changes.

In this chapter you will find information to help you understand various school policies and programs that frequently baffle parents.

School's Out "School's Out" is a weekly TV show produced by the staff of the Dunedin Elementary School just north of Clearwater, Florida. According to Mr. Richard Traylor, fifth grade teacher and producer of the show, the goal of "School's Out" is to bring the home and the school closer together by providing information for parents on school policies, programs, and procedures. They even offer suggestions about how parents can help their kids with schoolwork at home. Why not start such a program in your community? Parents can produce the show, run the cameras, and suggest topics they would like discussed.

Back to Basics

Q. I keep hearing people in our town talk about how our schools should get "back to basics." Yet when I ask people what they mean by "back to basics," everyone seems to have a different idea. What exactly is "back to basics" supposed to mean and where did the term come from?

A. The term was first coined in 1956 by the Council for Basic Education, a private organization of citizens concerned about education. At that time the notion of "life-adjustment educa-tion" was prevalent. Life-adjustment educators emphasized social growth and adjustment over the academic subjects in which it was felt many children could not succeed. Subjects like crafts and sewing and growing vegetables and consumer education were given status equal to traditional academic sub-jects such as reading and math and social studies. This empha-sis on non-academic study flourished in the sixties, when kids in school demanded "relevancy" in their courses and greater control over how their school day would be spent.

The Council for Basic Education in 1956 wanted schools to return to the more academic subjects of reading, writing, arithmetic, science, and social studies. Today the same council adds music, art, and foreign languages to this list of basic subject areas. The council recommends a shift in priorities that would reestablish the emphasis on academic subjects, thus getting "back to basics."

From that original meaning of the phrase come all of the other connotations of the term today. Some schools facing declining enrollment and declining budgets have latched on to the phrase as a justification for cutbacks in all programs except reading, writing, and arithmetic. Music, art, even science and social studies, are deemed "frills," subjects both costly and non-essential, and are therefore slashed from the budget.

The phrase is also used today to refer to a return to the strict school atmosphere of the forties and fifties. Often called "traditional schools" or "back-to-basics schools," these schools adopt strict behavior and dress codes. Girls wear skirts. Children walk through the halls silently and in straight lines. Wrongdoers are punished.

In many back-to-basics schools, even the style of teaching is drawn from earlier days. Gone are the learning centers and the hands-on learning projects so popular in the last two dec-ades. Instead, the emphasis is on sitting still, listening quietly to the teacher, and learning by drill, memorization, and frequent tests. Many critics feel that this kind of education does not prepare adults to think for themselves, to solve problems creatively, or to adjust to the rapid changes in today's world.

Being against "back to basics" today is like being against apple pie and motherhood. However, when carried to extremes that involve the return to anachronistic and limited programs, this movement can cost too much in loss of creativity and open-mindedness to be worth the gain in dollars and discipline.

Making Magnet Schools

Q. Our school district is currently planning to establish a "magnet school" for kids in grades 1–4 next September. All parents in the district can choose whether to send their kids to this magnet school or to the local neighborhood school. I don't really understand why the district needs to set up another program when it already has difficulty raising enough tax money to fund the schools and programs now in operation. What's the advantage of a magnet school? Should I send my children?

A. It goes without saying that children are not all alike. Yet the vast majority of school districts in America operate as if the differences between children don't exist. All children of the same age in the same grade are expected to learn the three R's at basically the same rate using the same materials. Differences in temperament and in learning styles are rarely accounted for. The needs, wishes, and desires of the parents concerning how and what their children will be taught are given no more than token consideration. More and more parents are transferring their kids from public schools to private schools and pushing Congress to grant tuition tax credits to ease the financial burden on parents who choose to do so.

The creation of magnet schools is an attempt by school

districts to meet the differing needs of children and the differing desires of parents. A magnet school follows a significantly different educational program from the other schools in the district. Any child is allowed to attend, regardless of the "school zone" in which the parents happen to reside. Thus the school is like a magnet, drawing in children from all over the district. In so doing, the district hopes to provide an educational setting where children of different racial and socio-economic levels mix. Sounds good in theory, but in practice these schools often draw very similar kinds of kids from very similar kinds of backgrounds.

There are many ways in which a magnet school program can differ from other district programs. Some magnet schools offer an open education program, which emphasizes learning by doing and allows the children to make many choices concerning what and how they learn. Some magnet schools are back-to-basics schools, which focus heavily on the basic skills of reading, writing, and arithmetic and have strong dress and behavior codes. Other magnet schools emphasize the arts or multi-cultural experiences. The type of program a district decides to offer usually reflects pressure from a strong group of local parents who want a certain educational experience for their children.

Why would parents choose to send their child to a magnet school? Perhaps the parents agree philosophically with the program being offered, and thus see the opportunity as a welcome change from the neighborhood school that is not to the parents' liking. Perhaps the child is doing poorly in the neighborhood school, either because of academic or behavior problems, and a change of school represents a new chance to succeed. Perhaps the child is unmotivated at present, and the parents feel a different program with different kids and different teachers will stimulate the child.

School districts are more likely to satisfy the differing needs of many kids and parents when options are offered. A magnet school program is one way a district can choose to offer such options.

Charging Fees for Programs

Q. The local school board wants to charge students for pencils, workbooks, and materials for shop and home economics next year. I'm already paying much more for school lunch than I did last year, and for field trips that used to be free. When will it stop? I pay my school taxes each year—shouldn't that be enough to cover the kids' education? Aren't my kids guaranteed free schooling by law?

A. It is true that each state guarantees children a free education. No tuition may be charged for daytime attendance at a public school during the regular school year. But what is included in that free education varies from state to state depending upon how the state's educational code is written. Thus we end up with situations in which fees for certain school services or functions are legal in one state but illegal in the next.

I predict you'll find more fees in the future for different services schools once provided for free. In past years voters all over the country have been defeating school budget after school budget. Their message is clear. They aren't willing to keep paying higher and higher taxes to support education, especially if the local district provides programs many people consider "frills."

Many taxpayers who vote no on school budgets support the idea of user fees as a way of continuing certain options in the schools but not spreading the burden of paying for those options to everyone. Such fees require the students involved in certain activities to pay all or part of the cost. These activities might be field trips, summer school, athletic programs, clubs. The list goes on and on. Some districts already have user fees for textbooks, pencils and paper, and others are even considering charging for transportation.

The Home Bulletin   Teachers at Sawyer Junior High School in Cincinnati, Ohio, publish "The Home Bulletin" each month. This newsletter focuses on activities and accomplishments of the school's staff and students. There's no reason why a group of parents in any school couldn't publish such a newsletter. Why not expand the coverage to include information on parent activities and accomplishments. You might even find a local business that is willing to donate printing facilities as a public service.

There are obvious problems with school fees. In this age of unemployment, some families will have trouble scraping together the required dollars. Certainly the gap will widen between those who can pay and those who can't. Educational opportunities will be increasingly unequal. It will be harder for low-income students to remain excited and motivated in school when desirable activities may be closed to them because of cost. Some students will find themselves torn between wanting to take part in school activities and not wanting to burden their parents. For these students, dropping out might be too easy a solution.

Any district that institutes fees should make the policy as fair as possible to all students and provide some sort of waiver for students who lack funds.

Reviewing School Records

Q.   I'm upset about something that happened when my husband and I went to my daughter's school last week for a conference. While the teacher talked to us, she kept referring frequently to a large folder on her lap that she said contained all of our child's school records. My husband and I asked if we could look through the folder ourselves. The teacher said no, that it was better if she summarized and interpreted the reports for us. What type of reports do teachers keep on file and why shouldn't parents be allowed to read them?

A.   Not only isn't it right for parents to be denied access to all the reports in their child's school folder, it's not legal. The Family Educational Rights and Privacy Act of 1974 contains many provisions which clearly spell out parents' rights regarding their child's school records.

First, parents have the right to inspect all school records pertaining to their child. This includes reports, test scores, psychological evaluations, and so on. Parents also have the right to ask the school for a copy of any or all of these records. The school may legally charge a duplicating fee. When a student turns eighteen, the above right is extended to the student.

Second, *only* parents have these rights. Before this law was enacted, prospective employers, court officials, and welfare workers could inspect a student's records. Not any longer.

Third, parents have the right to challenge any information found in the folder that they consider inaccurate or irrelevant to their child's education, and to ask that this information be removed. Sometimes teachers' reports contain subjective opinions about a child's potential or personality, or references to the lifestyle or beliefs of a child's parents. Opinions not substantiated by any factual material are clearly irrelevant, yet are often found in folders. It is important to make sure that any inaccurate or irrelevant material is removed from the folder, because a teacher's expectation of how a child will behave may be based on these records. Studies have shown that if a teacher expects a child to do poorly, the child usually will live up to this expectation, no matter what his or her potential.

Should school officials not comply with a request to remove information from a file, parents may request a hearing with an impartial hearing officer. Should this officer rule against the parent and the decision is made to leave the material in question in the student's folder, the only resource parents have is to place in the file a statement containing their objections to the information in question.

The following is a list of the information that should be in your child's folder:

• Statistical information, including the student's name, address, date of birth, parents' names, and places of business
• Attendance records
• Health information, including a record of screenings by the school nurse and any special health history or needs that would affect day-to-day schooling
• Cumulative achievement records, including teacher evaluations, grades, standardized test scores
• Unacceptable behavior reports and a record of disciplinary action taken, if any
• Reports by school specialists, such as reading teachers, social workers, psychologists, or speech teachers, if any of these specialists have seen or tested your child

The next time you go to a parent-teacher conference, ask to see the folder. If you don't understand the information or find any information lacking, ask for an explanation. You have a right to know.

Entering Kindergarten Early

Q. I assumed that my son would attend kindergarten next year until I was told that the cutoff date is December 1—just a few days before his fifth birthday. I've received conflicting information about whether or not schools make exceptions to this rule. Is advanced placement possible? Do you recommend it? My child will already have attended two years of nursery school and seems to show a natural interest in numbers and letters. I feel that he will be ready mentally and emotionally, although it is hard for me to judge objectively. How should I go about getting advanced placement if it is possible? If not, what type of preschool program do you recommend as an alternative?

A. Kindergarten programs are not mandated by federal law, and it is each state's decision whether or not to offer kindergarten classes. If such programs are offered, the state also determines the cutoff date for admission. This is the date by which the child must have reached his or her fifth birthday, although many states delegate these decisions to the local school districts. The cutoff dates vary from September 1 to January 1. If a child's birthday is after the cutoff date, even by just one or two days, he must wait an entire year before attending kindergarten.

Many school districts are flexible and allow early admission to kindergarten for such a child. The decision on early admission is usually made by school district officials based on a battery of tests administered by a school psychologist or counselor. Call your district's pupil personnel director or superintendent to find out if the district has an early admissions policy and, if so, who is in charge of the program.

Parents shouldn't be surprised, however, if they are discouraged from requesting early admission. The testing is done on a one-to-one basis and is time consuming. Also, schools are apprehensive of parents who want their kid in school not because it is necessarily best for the child but because it fits parental needs for day-care or desires for status.

Yet, in many cases, early admission does fit the child's need. If you feel your child might be ready, talk it over with the nursery school teachers who should be able to evaluate your child more objectively than you can. Ask them if your child appears to have reached a five-year-old's developmental level intellectually, socially, and emotionally. Have them assess his readiness skills in reading, writing, and arithmetic, along with large and small muscle coordination, independence, ability to follow directions, and willingness to cooperate with other children.

If they perceive that your son lags in any of these areas, it's best to wait another year. It can be detrimental to push a child too far, too soon. While he may succeed academically, he may always have to strive a little too much to keep up. Frustration can mount and friendships may be difficult to form and to sustain. Self-esteem can suffer. Consider, too, some of the advantages of waiting. Your son would be one of the oldest kids in the class next year. Older classmates tend to be the leaders, and mastering the lessons is often a bit easier for them. As they experience early school successes, self-confidence rises, paving the way for future achievement. Later in life, a difference in age of five or six months is meaningless. But in the early years as a child develops, these few months can make a huge difference.

If, however, the teachers feel that your child is ready in all areas, ask them to put their assessment in writing. Send the assessment, along with your written request for early kindergarten admission, to the person who administers the early-entrance program.

If it turns out that your son is to spend another year in nursery school, find a program that provides early academic experiences through material well suited to the young child. These early learning experiences should be individual, not group instruction, and should be in addition to the usual nursery school play activities.

Full Day for Five-Year-Olds

Q. My daughter is going to an all-day kindergarten this year. All of our other children only went to kindergarten for a couple of hours in the morning, and I'm not sure a five-year-old is ready to be in school all day. The school says the kids are better prepared for first grade if they go to an all-day kindergarten. Do you think this is true?

A. It depends upon the kindergarten program. A good all-day program is an advantage for most children. It's especially advantageous for the children of working mothers who have already been in day-care centers and pre-kindergartens before they are five and thus are already used to being away from home for the full day. It is bewildering for these children to go to kindergarten for only a few hours and then to go to a different program for the afternoon. They would fare much better in one place for the entire day.

Indeed, studies have shown that the five-year-old is ready for more academic and intellectual learning than the usual half-day program provides. It is crucial, however, for the teaching to suit the learning style of five-year-olds, which is different from the style of a six- or seven-year-old. Schools that ignore this important fact make the mistake of having kindergarten children do reading and math activities in groups and fill out workbooks. Instead, five-year-olds should work individually, at their own pace, with concrete learning materials that are manipulative, self-correcting, and can be repeated over and over until the child has mastered the task. Only then should the child move to the next, more difficult task. These materials should be so attractive to the child that learning becomes an enjoyable activity, not a dreary task to be hurriedly completed in order to get to more interesting non-academic activities. Many such materials are on the market today.

Along with the academic learning that lays a solid foundation for future reading, writing, and arithmetic activities, all-day kindergarten programs still need to offer the child the same chances for social and emotional growth that half-day programs did. There must be "free time" during which the child chooses his or her own activities and playmates. There must also be blocks, sand tables, painting corners, cut-and-paste activities, etc., to foster the child's creativity and artistic development.

One of the biggest advantages of an all-day kindergarten program is that the teacher only has to work with approximately twenty-five children instead of fifty. This allows the teacher to really get to know your child and to be able to offer whatever specific help and guidance is needed. Knowing fifty children in depth simply isn't possible—some kids get lost in the shuffle. Knowing fifty sets of parents well isn't possible, either. Expect the teacher in an all-day kindergarten program to have more time to conference with each parent, thus keeping you better informed about your child's progress.

How Johnny Learns to Read

Q. Our daughter is entering first grade in the fall. I know very little about schools since she is our oldest child. I'm particularly concerned about whether or not she will learn to read successfully, since I had much difficulty learning to read when I was in school. I'm also worried that she'll get turned off to reading because the stories in the readers young kids are given seem so dull to me, as dull as the Dick and Jane stories I was given. How can I tell if a first grade reading program is good?

A. Your daughter's reading program will probably look very different from the one used when you attended school. There are a great many different reading programs in use today, but the best programs share certain characteristics.

The basic approach to reading has changed over the past generation. When you were in school most kids learned to read by the "look-say" method. Children memorized a specific set of words and then read stories that used these words.

Today the emphasis in beginning reading is on phonics, on learning the relationship between letters and sounds. Kids are taught to sound out words rather than to memorize them.

Stories are comprised of words that the children should be able to sound out. The irregular words in English, which cannot be sounded out, are memorized.

Obviously, with the phonics approach, early readers have to be very simple and contain only words with sound patterns that have already been taught: "The fat cat sat on a rat" is an example. The meaning in these early phonetic stories is minimal at best. Yet the phonetic approach is very useful for most beginning readers, and should not be thrown out in the quest for more interesting or meaningful content.

Today's reading programs usually have a clear scope and sequence of skills to be taught, not only in first grade but in every grade level. Teachers have handy charts printed by the textbook publishers that outline these skills. If you want to know the specifics of your daughter's program, ask to see these charts.

You'll also want to find out what method the teacher uses to determine whether or not your child has learned the skills being taught and what plans are made if she has not mastered them. Does the teacher reteach any skills not mastered, or will the child be moved ahead to the next skill regardless, thus acquiring a very weak foundation on which to build her reading ability?

Today children usually learn to read in small groups, rather than in large classes. Find out what the basis of the grouping is in her school, and how flexible this grouping is.

Besides teaching the mechanics of reading, a good first-grade program must also motivate the child to want to read. The real problem with the stories in early readers is not that they are unimaginative but that reading instruction is often limited only to the mechanics of reading and thus to the material in the primers.

All through elementary school, most children are able to comprehend and enjoy stories that are way beyond their reading ability level. Children's love of reading is stimulated when adults, including teachers, librarians, and parents read these stories aloud to them and share their own joy and enthusiasm for the stories. These are the stories that should be discussed in detail in classes. When a child senses that the reward for mastering the mechanics of reading is the ability to read his favorite stories, his motivation to learn to read goes sky high.

Both teachers and parents need to promote the use of the school library. Library books, newspapers, and magazines written especially for children should be as much a part of a child's daily reading program as the teaching of reading mechanics. Book displays should be set up around the room and changed frequently. Some teachers even model the behavior they want to encourage by keeping a book that they are currently reading on a corner of their desk so the children become aware that the teacher also reads for pleasure and for information.

Most important of all, in a good reading program the teacher has high expectations for each child. Teachers who believe that all children can learn, no matter what their family background or early experiences, usually produce classes of good readers.

Encourage the Student Teacher

Q. Most of our son's reading program is now being taught by a student teacher. We're not sure we like the idea because we suspect this student does not have the same qualifications as our son's regular teacher, whom we like very much. We realize students have to practice somewhere, but how can we be sure our child's learning doesn't suffer because of it?

A. Before a prospective teacher can be licensed he or she must have at least one supervised, on-the-job teaching experience. The student teacher is really a pre-professional supervised both by the classroom teacher to whom he or she is assigned and by an instructor from the college where he or she studies. The classroom teacher retains full responsibility for what happens in the classroom and must make sure that no child's learning suffers during this process. Usually only the most highly qualified and successful classroom teachers are assigned student teachers.

Most kids benefit when there is a student teacher in their classroom. With two adults in the room they get much more individual attention and instruction. Projects and trips can be planned that one person couldn't handle alone. The idealism and enthusiasm that many student teachers have about teaching and about kids can spark the entire class.

You can help both the student teacher and your child get the most out of this experience. Part of the student's training is to learn to deal with parents. Since you probably have had more experience dealing with teachers than he or she has had with parents, it is your job to initiate and maintain personal contact.

Discuss with your child how he feels about the student teacher. State your expectation that he will respect and listen to this teacher just as he does his regular teacher. Your enthusiasm about his two teachers and your own personal contact with the student teacher will provide him with a good role model for his own attitude.

Should difficulties arise between your child and the student teacher, or should you have any concern that your child's learning is being jeopardized, ask for a conference with both teachers to discuss the problem and to plan any changes that seem necessary in your child's program.

Tales Textbooks Tell

Q. My husband and I spent part of last weekend reading one of our son's sixth grade textbooks. We found the book to be boring and out-of-date. Many of the issues to which we think a twelve-year-old should be exposed to were hardly touched upon. Should we take our complaints about the book to his teacher or is the principal responsible for textbook selection?

A. By all means take your complaints to both the teacher and the principal—it's important that they know how you feel. But don't be surprised if they both tell you that they have no control over the book your son is using.

The procedure by which textbooks are chosen varies from state to state and district to district. In some states, known as "adoption" states, a central agency chooses textbooks for use in all districts; only such "approved" textbooks may be used. The central agency might adopt just one sixth grade social studies textbook or they might approve three or four texts and let each district choose from the approved list. If a limited choice is given, the district might have its own committee to choose which book to use, or it might give the choice to the principals or teachers involved.

Other states, known as "open states," have no such central agency and leave textbook selection completely in the hands of each school district. The district can then delegate responsibility in the ways described above. To find out the policy in your state, ask the superintendent of schools, the school principal, a PTA officer, or a member of the Board of Education.

The lack of in-depth treatment of important issues is a feature of many textbooks. Textbook publishers are in business to make money, not to expose kids to complex and controversial issues. They take great pains to see that their books are not offensive to any special interest group that might lobby to have the book rejected by their local school district or state. Obviously, a lot of profit is involved when a text is chosen for an entire state by a central committee. So publishers put a lot of emphasis on sales to adoption states, which results in the glossing over of many important issues.

So, depending upon the selection procedures of your state and district, complaining may be all you can do about your son's book. If there is a local selection committee, by all means register your complaint with them.

In addition, you can make it a parental responsibility to expose your son to other social studies books more to your liking. The young adult's section of the public library has many excellent books of all levels of sophistication on almost any topic you could want. Make a family visit to the library and ask the librarian to help you find these books. It could become a family project for everyone to read these books and participate in dinner-table discussions of the issues. Yes, it's more time-consuming to look into these issues as a family if your child isn't learning them in school, but in the long run it's also more rewarding.

Kids Teaching Kids

Q. I received a note from my daughter's teacher requesting my permission for her to read stories to kindergarten children three days a week. Frankly, my daughter, who is in fifth grade, isn't such a good reader herself. I think she needs someone older to tutor and read to her more than she needs to help younger kids. Do you think I should give my permission?

A. By all means! Sign the permission slip and return it to the teacher at once.

Older children are chosen to read to kindergarten children to accomplish two things:
• to benefit the kindergarten children, who will have someone available to read stories to individuals and small groups while their teacher is busy doing something else. Most five-year-olds have a voracious appetite for stories—older children can help satisfy this desire.
• to benefit the older child. I'll make a bet your daughter's

teacher specifically chose her for this opportunity in order to boost her reading performance and to raise her self-esteem.

It's not hard to see how reading to a younger child can boost your daughter's reading skills. She will have to pre-read and prepare the stories she will be reading aloud. That means extra reading practice, practice with books that she might not read otherwise because she thinks they are too babyish for her. That means learning to read with expression. The school librarian or an aide often helps the older tutor prepare by listening to him or her read the story aloud, and offering suggestions for increased expression. In addition, having positive experiences with books just might increase her own motivation to read for pleasure, something poor readers don't often choose to do.

The boost to your daughter's self-esteem will be just as important as the academic benefits. Your daughter will feel capable because she is able to perform a task satisfactorily. The younger kids will look up to her and admire her. She will feel useful and needed, as it will be obvious the kindergarten children wouldn't get a chance to hear these stories if it weren't for her. She will learn to be dependable as it becomes clear to her how much the kids look forward to her visits. And she will learn to prepare in advance for important activities.

Schools that set up programs that encourage older children to help younger kids do so because of the great benefits such tutoring provides for both children. Your daughter is fortunate to be able to participate in such a program.

Repeating Papers Prepares Kids

Q. I save papers that my kids bring home from school. As I browsed through a large stack of math sheets done by my second-grader recently, I noticed that some of the assignments had been repeated four or five times. Most of the problems on the repeated papers were correct, so I don't understand why my daughter repeated the same work instead of moving ahead to the next step. Why should she be wasting her time practicing what she already knows?

A. If your child repeats math worksheets instead of moving forward to the next steps when she is ready, you have a problem. If she repeats them in addition to moving forward, no problem exists. You might be able to tell what is happening by placing the sheets in dated sequence and looking to see if new concepts are being introduced on a regular basis.

Most children, and adults too, reap great pleasure from repeating their successes. Self-confidence rises from the knowledge that what was once unknown now has been mastered and can be performed with ease.

The most likely explanation for the duplicate worksheets is that her teacher runs off extra copies and puts them on a shelf in the back of the classroom for kids to take and do when their day's assignments have been completed. It's amazing to see how eagerly many children voluntarily complete these extra worksheets. Yet these same kids complain vigorously about other worksheets that are assigned for the day!

The explanation for this seemingly contradictory behavior may surprise you. Assigned worksheets are greeted with groans because the kids are being *told* what to do; the repeated worksheets are viewed as treats because the kids have *chosen* what to do. No one is telling them they must do them. No pressure is being applied. Choice, coupled with the good feeling of repeated success, motivates many children to do the extra work.

Artist's Abilities Aren't Appreciated

Q. I'm afraid my eight-year-old son's artistic abilities are being stifled in school. He loves to draw and paint and seems creative in what he produces, mixing colors and designs in different and interesting ways. In school, the teacher plans the art project for the entire class and the children must follow her directions exactly. Everyone ends up producing the same thing. The teacher sends notes, saying that he is uncooperative and refuses to follow directions. He says he wants to create something different. I think the teacher is wrong and is actually interfering with my son's artistic development. Talking to her has not helped the situation. What next?

A. Since talking to the teacher did not help, talk to your son instead. Explain that "art" is defined differently by different people. For him, art is a creative, imaginative process; for his teacher, art is following directions to produce something. If he accepts these differences, performs as expected in class, and receives encouragement and support for developing his talent elsewhere, the teacher's definition of art and the activities she provides for the class need not inhibit his creative processes.

Encourage him by supplying a wide range of artistic materials for him to use at home. Perhaps there are art classes in the community that stress individual talent and creativity. Share his interest by visiting museums and galleries with him and talking and reading about what you see there. Explore the many wonderful books on art at the public library.

Computers Come into Classrooms

Q. I'm not writing about my own kids—they are all grown with kids of their own. I'm writing about other people's kids and the money it costs to educate them today. I don't mind schools spending money on teaching reading and writing, but when it comes to spending my tax money to buy computers for the kids to play with, I draw the line. My education was perfectly adequate—without computers. Wouldn't it be nice if schools didn't always want more of anything and everything that comes on the market?

A. A decade ago parents complained they couldn't help their children with their "new math" homework. Today's parents are just as frustrated trying to understand the computer programs kids as young as seven and eight are learning to write in school. Many parents, and especially grandparents, have an inaccurate perception of the use and importance of computers in schools today.

Computers are not a frill or just for playing games. In schools, computers form the bridge to the future world which today's youngsters will inhabit.

I foresee a time in the not-too-distant future when computer competency will be a requirement for a high-school diploma, just as reading and math competency is required in many states today. For significant numbers of today's kids, the ability to use a computer will mean the difference between employment and unemployment, a well-paying job and a poorly paying one.

Computers not only play games; they also teach. Computers can provide drill and reinforcement for learning basic skills. Computers can also individualize instruction, allowing the slower student extra practice and providing enrichment for the quick learner.

But that's not all. Computers stimulate and motivate many kids to learn. Fascinated by the machines, the kids will often come to school early and stay late just for the chance to use them. Recent studies indicate that kids learn to program and master computers with no more difficulty than the average adult. Mastery of a machine as complicated as a computer boosts any child's self-esteem and self-confidence. Membership in a school's computer club yields benefits equal to participating on an athletic team, and for the non-athletic child, here is a chance to belong and be accepted in a positive way.

The real issue is not whether or not computers belong in the schools. The question is how they will be financed and how access to computers will be equalized for all children.

Boys and Girls Together

Q. In my daughter's school all the gym classes are coed. She is in the sixth grade now and doesn't like having gym with the boys. She says they make fun of the girls, and that the boys always win when they have games against each other. I've asked the principal why they don't have separate classes like we did when I went to school. He says that now separate gym classes are illegal. Is this true?

A. Title IX of the Education Amendments of 1972 requires equal facilities and opportunities for boys and girls to participate in school sports programs, both for required physical education programs that take place during the school day and for after-school athletics. The law states that "No person in the United States shall, on the basis of sex, be excluded from participation in, or be denied the benefits of, or be subjected to discrimination under any educational program or activity receiving federal financial assistance."

The law has been interpreted to mean that boys and girls will participate in co-ed instruction during physical education periods. The only time they can be segregated is when they are playing contact sports such as football, basketball, wrestling, hockey, and so on. Baseball and kickball, which are often played in elementary schools, are not usually considered contact sports.

The law does allow what is known as ability grouping in non-contact athletics. Gym teachers and coaches may separate students not by sex but by their ability to play any given sport, as measured by some objective criteria applied to boys and girls alike. Since in any given sport there would be some boys who play well and others who play poorly, and some girls who play well and others who play poorly, it is likely that if the criterion is fairly applied one would not find all boys in one ability group and all girls in another, so classes would most likely be coed.

The problem your daughter is experiencing in gym class can be handled in other ways than by merely segregating the girls from the boys. A skillful teacher will help all the children become more sensitive and comfortable with each other.

First of all, it makes poor sense to always have girls' teams pitted against boys' teams. That kind of competition serves no useful purpose. Each team should be composed of boys and girls, good players and poor players. And the teams should change frequently so that everyone has a chance to win and lose occasionally and to play with everyone else. The teacher can teach the children how to handle both winning and losing. No one should be making fun of anyone else, regardless of gender.

Perhaps more time could be devoted to non-competitive athletic activities, too. Not everyone has the ability to be a superstar, and too often those with less ability find nothing of value in competitive team sports. School programs should be designed to promote physical fitness in all students, regardless of athletic ability.

Mix and Match in Middle Schools

Q. Schools are being reorganized in our community. In September my twelve- and fourteen-year-old daughters will be attending a middle school rather than a junior high school. School board members tell us that middle schools are better for youngsters than junior high schools, but I wonder if that's true. Is it just a name change or are middle schools really that much better?

A. The middle-school movement attempts to retain some of the characteristics of the elementary school while slowly introducing kids to the structure of high schools. Some middle schools contain grades 5–8, others 6–8, some have grades 6–9. The extent that this reorganization reflects a true change in educational practice and philosophy varies from city to city and from school to school.

This trend toward middle schools began with a realization that many fifth- and sixth-graders needed something different from what the elementary schools were offering, and that many ninth-graders were ready for the senior high program. At issue, too, was the fact that many kids fared poorly in the junior highs because the transition from elementary school into a totally different school program was too abrupt. Declining enrollment also plays a role in the move toward middle schools; as the number of students declines, school administrators like to close buildings in an attempt to save money. Regrouping the kids into middle schools eases this process and makes closing schools more palatable to a community.

Traditionally, junior high schools were training grounds for senior high schools. Seventh- and eighth-graders were considered too old to be in elementary school programs; ninth-graders seemed too young for senior high programs. So these youngsters were grouped together in an environment closely resembling high school. Every forty or fifty minutes, kids changed classes, and during the day they had six or seven different teachers. Teachers taught their own specialized areas of instruction. Since most teachers saw upward of 150 children daily, rarely could they give much individual attention or meet in groups to discuss the specific needs of certain youngsters.

In the middle schools, classes and teacher changes are limited to three or four a day, instead of six or seven, as in high school. This is accomplished by grouping teachers and children and organizing the curriculum into clusters of related studies rather than individual disciplines. Each group of teachers spends time together to plan and to discuss individual children's needs. More attention can be given to each student. Programs and resources can be modified and allocated to meet these needs.

With improved lab facilities for science courses, larger libraries, better equipped gyms and more emphasis on team sports, home economics, art areas, and even computer centers, middle schools also resemble high schools. Kids tend to have more academic choices and options than they have in elementary school. A different social atmosphere exists, too. There is more freedom to mix kids from different classes in the lunchroom, in study halls, and on the playground.

Thus, most middle schools are not just a name change, but a sincere effort by educators to design a program to better meet the needs of the youngsters they serve.

Coping with Careers

Q. My son is in the process of choosing electives for next year, his last in junior high school. One of the electives he can choose is called Career Education. Is this the same as the vocational education courses that teach kids a trade?

A. Some very basic differences exist between career education and vocational education. Vocational education courses can be very beneficial to the student who is not planning to attend college. Many students who find no value in regular high-school classes become motivated when given a chance to learn a skill or trade that interests them and that will lead to paid employment upon graduation.

Career education has the similar goal of preparing a student for the world of work. There the similarity ends, for the type of preparation offered is vastly different.

Career education does not teach specific skills. Rather, its goal is to teach students about the world of work. Students in career education courses explore many different occupations, finding out what the work is like, what kind of training is required, and what the future job prospects are for that occupation. Students also explore their own interests and talents, and are encouraged to see how these relate to the job marketplace.

Career education helps students make beginning decisions about what their future place in the world of work will be.

Career education is a necessity today. Gone are the days when children were expected to follow in the career footsteps of their parents. The revolution in technology has opened up many career opportunities that simply did not exist when we were making our own career decisions. Many fields that were traditionally considered only for men or women now have opened their doors to the opposite sex. The choice of a career has become and will continue to become increasingly complex, and career education in the schools is one attempt to help youngsters cope with that complexity.

Support the Substitute

Q. My daughter's teacher has been sick a lot this year. Consequently, her class is often being taught by a substitute teacher. When this happens the kids misbehave a lot. She also complains that she's bored because the substitute doesn't really "teach" anything, but just gives the kids a lot of busy-work to keep them quiet. Why does this happen? Who are the substitute teachers, what are their qualifications, and what can be done so that my daughter doesn't waste a day every time her teacher is out of school?

A. It is up to the education department of each state to set certification requirements for substitute teachers. In most cases, substitute teachers are certified classroom teachers with a bachelor's degree. Some even have a master's degree. Many are not substitutes by choice; they would much prefer to have their own classrooms. But since there is a surplus of teachers in a job market that is shrinking in most areas, there are not enough classroom teaching jobs to go around. So these teachers work on a day-to-day basis wherever they are needed, with hopes that they will be considered first for any full time openings in schools where they have substituted.

Other teachers are substitutes by choice. They don't want the full time responsibilities that a classroom entails, particularly the lesson planning, conferencing with parents, and faculty meetings. They are willing to accept less pay for less work. Perhaps they have other commitments and interests that require a good deal of time. They may be mothers who only want to be out of the home two or three days a week. Still others are older teachers not ready to retire completely but no longer willing or able to hold a full time classroom position.

It is the responsibility of the substitute to teach, not just to keep the kids busy. The lessons are all planned in advance by the regular classroom teacher, who should also leave notes on classroom organization and procedures. Sometimes a lesson is quicker than the plan says it should be, or it rains and a planned recess is canceled. Most people who sub a lot bring along extra activities, "fillers" to use with the kids when there is extra time. When used in addition to the planned lesson, these activities can be a pleasant break.

It is the principal's role to supervise substitute teachers, to see that plans have been left for them, and to make sure that the plans have been followed.

A number of factors contribute to the success of a substitute teacher. Of major importance is how well the classroom teacher has prepared her class for substitutes. The regular teacher needs to set up the expectation that the children will participate in the learning activities and will behave in an acceptable manner. Consequences for misbehavior must also be spelled out. The children must know that the substitute will report misbehavior so the classroom teacher can carry out the consequences.

Another factor in the success of a substitute is familiarity with the school and its programs and policies. Many schools have "regular" substitutes who know the programs and the kids. Some schools even allow teachers to request a particular substitute. These teachers make an effort to have the same person substitute for them each time they are out, thereby minimizing the disruption in the routine.

As a parent, you can do two things. First, state your own expectation to your kids that you expect them to learn and to behave with a substitute, just as if their teacher were present. Second, find out through your school's PTA or parent organization what your school's policies toward substitutes are. See if some of the success factors listed here are followed in your school. If not, use the parents' group to lobby for change in substitute policy.

10

• •

What Do I
Do Now?

Each of the previous chapters dealt with a specific topic concerning your child's education. This chapter is different. It is a potpourri of parents' frequently asked questions about all sorts of problems. The best way to handle most problems is to follow the basic principles incorporated throughout this book.

As much as is humanly possible, it's best to encourage kids to be responsible for their own behavior by experiencing the consequences of their actions. Parents try to stand by, serve as a sounding board when our kids need to talk things over, offer support and affection, but not to shield them from these consequences. Remember that childhood can't always be happy and that learning to deal with minor misfortunes—particularly those caused by the kids' own behavior—is an essential part of growing up.

We should take an active role in the schools by keeping ourselves informed concerning school-related issues, getting involved in parents' organizations, and establishing and maintaining close contact with teachers. We also know that when kids are included in the solution-finding process, their willingness to cooperate with parents and teachers increases.

Now let's see what actions you can take to solve some of the problems that arise in coping with kids and school.

Making Mornings Manageable

Q. Getting the kids up and ready for school on time is a task that will surely turn my hair gray before I reach thirty—if I live that long! Please, some hints on how to survive the hours between waking up in the morning and waving goodbye to the schoolbus.

A. Getting kids ready for school and out the door on time is a hassle that plagues many parents. The first step toward avoiding early morning unpleasantness is to realize that the following responsibilities belong to the kids:

- Getting up in the morning
- Choosing clothes and getting dressed
- Making sure bodies, hands, and faces are clean
- Remembering books, homework, lunch money, musical instruments, sneakers, etc.
- Preparing lunches.

If your kids don't have their own alarm clock, take them shopping and let them each choose one. Together decide what time to set the clock so there's enough time to dress and get ready for school before breakfast is served. Some children like to set their clocks earlier than parents think necessary because they like to move slowly in the morning. Other kids prefer to set the clock later and rush. These are legitimate decisions for kids to make.

Help kids in kindergarten and first grade pick out their school clothes before going to bed. Older children need no help. It's hard for many parents to let the kids pick out their own clothes, for many kids choose items or combinations that don't seem appropriate to their parents. What if a nine-year-old puts on short sleeves on a cold day? The natural consequence of being cold will teach him or her to choose more appropriately next time. If he or she dresses too warmly, he or she will learn to dress more lightly. Certain color combinations that look OK to the kids might irritate a parent; so might wearing a style a parent finds outlandish. Peer pressure to dress in one way is stronger than all the reasons you can give the kids to dress differently. Think of it this way. You'd look and feel as out of place with your friends dressed in clothes your kids like as they might look and feel dressed in clothes you like.

Set up a scheduled time for breakfast, lasting anywhere from twenty to thirty minutes. Choose a time that ends about fifteen minutes before the kids must leave the house for school. Breakfast is available to any child who arrives at the table completely washed, dressed, and ready for school. The dawdlers and complainers will find the only thing that happens if they don't meet their morning responsibilities is that they miss breakfast. The proper response of a parent to this child is, "I sure am sorry you missed breakfast this morning. Maybe tomorrow you'll make it on time." Remember, lectures and "I told you so's" are not helpful at this point. You must remain calm and friendly for consequences to be effective.

The kids won't starve if they miss a meal or two. Though their morning performance in school might suffer, it is a temporary situation lasting only until they learn that unpleasant consequences occur when they don't fulfill their responsibilities.

Kids will stop forgetting lunch money, sneakers, homework, etc. soon after parents stop reminding and remembering for them. Ever notice that the more you remind, nag, threaten or scold a kid, the less they do what you want? Worse than reminding them is remembering for them. If kids who forget things call home and mom or dad brings the items to school, there's no consequence for forgetting, and no reason to remember. The child who has to go through the day without certain books, or who has to repeat an assignment during recess because the homework is on the kitchen table, or who sits on the sidelines during gym because forgotten sneakers are under the bed will have powerful incentives to learn the art of remembering.

Parent Hotlines Join with other parents to form a parent hotline to provide information and reassurance for troubled parents in your neighborhood. One parent may need a sympathetic ear while he or she vents frustration about a school-related problem. Another may want information about how to approach a teacher with a concern, or may want another parent's opinion on how to handle a homework problem. Just knowing that such help is available is comforting to many parents. Use the school newsletter to publish the phone numbers of parents who are willing to provide this service for other parents. Rotate the numbers frequently.

Kids who bring lunch to school can make it themselves. Some parents prefer to have a sandwich jamboree once a week and freeze the sandwiches for easy packing each day. Others have kids make and pack their bags the night before. Some set the alarm clocks a little earlier in the morning so that there will be time then. Choose the plan that makes the most sense to you. The important factor is that the kids pack their own lunches. *And* clean up the mess afterward.

New routines and responsibilities for the kids require a settling in period during which kids test the limits, blow their responsibilities, and experience the unpleasant consequences that result. Don't give in to either complaints or expressions of unhappiness. Apply the limits firmly and with consistency. Your reward will be decreased hassles in the months to come. Your kids' reward will be more self-confidence because they have learned to take care of their own needs.

School Bus Versus Family Bus

Q. My kids, ten, thirteen, and fifteen, hate to ride the school bus. They say it takes too long, but I would think they'd like being with their friends on the way to and from school. And it's a lot more convenient for me than driving them myself. Do other parents have this problem?

A. Many kids object to amount of time they must spend on the bus to ride a relatively short distance. Depending upon your geographical location, the morning bus pick-up time may be before daylight. This is no treat, especially in cold weather. There may be a long walk to the bus stop, too, which is not very pleasant if it's dark and cold outside.

Many kids also object to the rowdy behavior of some of the other kids on the bus. Keeping order on a school bus is not an easy job. If parents and teachers experience difficulty disciplining children effectively, imagine the poor bus driver.

Discuss the situation with your children. They may be able to find ways to reduce the inconvenience you face should you drive them yourself. They might be willing to get up early enough to prepare and clean up after breakfast, saving you time. They might lend a hand in the afternoon to make up for the time you spend driving. If agreements can be reached that satisfy everyone, then riding together in the mornings and afternoons might just become a very pleasant time for everyone.

On the other hand, don't feel guilty if, after discussing the situation, you decide that riding the school bus is really the best way for the kids to get to school. Your kids will learn to survive the inconveniences and unpleasantness riding a school bus often entails. They might even find ways to make the trip enjoyable.

Lessons Learned from Lunches Left

Q. I'm annoyed because the school secretary won't let my son call me when he's forgotten his weekly lunch money. I'd be glad to drive over to the school and give it to him—that's a lot easier than having to pack his sandwiches for the entire following week. Do you know how I can pressure the school into changing its policy on kids calling home?

A. Sorry, but this time the school secretary is taking appropriate action. If every child who forgot his lunch money was allowed to call home, the school secretary's phone line would be tied up all morning.

More important, however, is that calling home and having mom or dad bring the lunch money teaches a child an unfortunate lesson in irresponsibility and forgetfulness. Why bother to remember lunch money each week if there's no penalty for forgetting it?

The job of remembering lunch money belongs to each kid, not to his parents. Mark the day that the money is due on either a family calendar or your child's individual calendar. Suggest to your son that he put the lunch money in his bookbag or pants pocket the night before it is due, so the money is not forgotten in the morning confusion and rush. Don't spend the next morning nagging and reminding him about the lunch money; there often seems to be a direct correlation between the amount of nagging a parent does and the amount of forgetting a child does.

Be sure that the consequences of forgetting lunch money fall on your son, not on you, or the lesson in responsibility will be lost. That means he makes the sandwiches when they are needed, not you.

Should he forget to bring his homemade lunch to school, he goes without lunch for a day. Don't bring it to him. He won't starve.

Allow these small responsibilities to belong to your son. It's a marvelous way to prepare him for the larger responsibilities that he'll face later on.

On Giving Lunch Away

Q. When my eight-year-old son comes home from school I ask him what he ate for lunch. Every day the answer is almost the same. "I wasn't hungry," he'll say, "so I gave my sandwich to Jimmy." Or, "I traded my sandwich and cheese for a candy bar." It's important to me that he eat good food. He knows I get upset when he doesn't eat what I pack for him. This scenario spoils our afternoon together and, when the first thing we do each day after school is argue about lunch, the unpleasantness seems to last the rest of the day. I can't give in because I know he'll work better in school in the afternoons if he eats a nutritious lunch. How can I make him understand this?

A. Your intentions are excellent. Good nutrition is important for children. However, the way you go about influencing your son's eating habits is doomed to failure. Asking and fighting with him daily obviously isn't helping and probably is creating negative feelings that taint your entire relationship.

End these afternoon scenes immediately by saying nothing about lunch. Instead, when he returns from school, talk about his day and yours. Look at any work or books he's brought home from school. Have a nutritious snack together. Make this a pleasant, conflict-free time. The first few minutes after a child returns home set the entire tone for the rest of the day.

You cannot control what your child eats in school, nor are you there to enforce limits or consequences. Your child knows your threats are empty because the only way you can know what he eats is by what he tells you. He can decide to tell you he ate everything you wanted him to eat and then do exactly as he pleases.

Influence his eating habits by providing only nutritious foods for breakfast, snacks, and supper. Give him control over lunches by letting him decide whether to buy the school lunch or to pack his own. If he takes lunch, let him plan it and fix it himself. When he exercises more control over his lunches, and when you stop making a major issue over them each afternoon, he'll be more likely to do just what you wanted all along—eat a nutritious lunch.

Switching Teachers

Q. This school year has started badly for my daughter. She's unhappy with her teacher and has asked me to talk to the principal about having her switched to a different classroom. I'm not sure whether I should do this, or whether it would be better to let her learn to live with the situation.

A. Sooner or later every child is faced with a teacher he or she doesn't like. In elementary schools, where a child often has only one teacher all day, this can be a tough situation. Even so, you'll find most principals reluctant to move a child to a different classroom. Thus the most productive role for you is to help your daughter learn how to cope with this situation and even to gain from it.

If your daughter were to switch to a different classroom, she would simply be running away from the problem. The hidden message in such a change is "You can't solve the problem, so we'll do it for you by removing you from the situation." Even when a child has asked for it this causes self-confidence to go down and feelings of helplessness and powerlessness to grow.

The first step toward helping your daughter deal with this situation is to listen to her talk about her teacher. Encourage her to say everything she is thinking and feeling. Don't use this occasion to pass judgments, criticize, give advice, and so on. Just listen and reflect back to her the feelings you hear her expressing. This will help her feel that you understand what she is experiencing, help her clarify her feelings, and pinpoint exactly what bothers her. Avoid taking sides while you listen—doing so will only make it harder for your daughter to cope with the problem.

Don't Legislate Feelings   Never tell kids how they *should* feel about something. Never say "You don't really feel that way" when they tell you how they feel. When you try to legislate and control kids' feelings, they become confused and disoriented and learn to mistrust their own perceptions of the world. Instead, listen to their feelings, share their feelings. When appropriate, perhaps even state your own different feelings about the matter at hand.

Wait a few days before you suggest the next step—talking to the teacher. Many problems, no matter how drastic they seem at the time, are transient. An unpleasant incident in class today, which results in an emotional outburst at home tonight, may be forgotten by next week.

If the problem persists for a week or two, suggest a talk with the teacher. The older and more mature the child is, the greater the chance that the child can handle this talk alone. Being able to face the teacher without a parent at her side will raise your child's feelings of competency. It may help for you to rehearse the talk at home. You play the teacher and let your daughter practice what she is going to say. Go with your daughter if you feel she is too young or insecure to handle the conference alone.

The purpose of talking with the teacher is twofold. The child needs to express her feelings, and both teacher and child need to set some steps that can be taken to help the child feel better about being in the class. It's a problem solving conference.

The perfect solution may not exist. Your daughter needs to know that through the years she will probably have to face and cope with a number of teachers she doesn't like. Explain to her that liking the teacher, or not being liked by the teacher, is not a prerequisite for successful learning. When she learns to make the best of a less-than-perfect situation, she learns an important life skill.

Forced into Fighting

Q. My eight-year-old is having trouble. Other kids often bully him on the way home from school, kicking and punching as he walks by. I want my kids to solve problems with words, not fists. I don't believe in telling kids that it's okay to fight. Why should he come down to their level? He says that because he doesn't fight back the other kids tease him even more and call him names like "sissy" and "scaredy cat." How can I teach him to defend himself without resorting to bully behavior?

A. Let's differentiate between aggressive and defensive fighting. It's important to teach our children to attempt to solve disagreements with words and negotiation. Unfortunately, there are times when other kids initiate fights. We can teach our kids to attempt to solve these situations with words and negotiation, too. However, should they encounter situations when such attempts fail, it's important that we give our children permission to defend themselves physically. Many parents even enroll their kids in martial arts classes so that, should the situation arise, their kids will have the skills to defend themselves.

Should the problem continue more than a couple of weeks, talk it over with the school principal. Ask your son if other children experience similar difficulties with the same bullies. If so, ask their parents to join you. School principals are in a good position to gather all the kids together in order to find ways to prevent these fights.

This is one of those times when it's okay to intervene on your child's behalf, to set a process in motion that will look for solutions to a difficult situation. However, if your child often finds himself in situations from which he needs to be rescued, continued parental intervention may only make matters worse. In such a case, counseling may be needed to help him understand the role he plays in such situations, the payoffs he gets, and ways he can act to avoid the problem.

Adjusting to a New School

Q. We moved to a new state over the summer. My nine-year-old daughter loved the school she was attending. And she's already expressed negative feelings about her new school. What can I do to make the transition easier on her?

A. When you visit the new school to register your daughter, take her with you. While you are there, find out everything you can about this new school environment. Remember to bring along all records and reports from previous schools, including health records, so she can be appropriately placed in a classroom. If she received any supportive services in the previous school, such as speech or remedial-reading instruction, request that these services be continued. Be prepared to give the school information about where you can be reached in case of an emergency.

Ask: What are the school hours? What supplies are expected from home? How much does school lunch cost and when is the money collected? Are menus provided so choices can be made ahead of time? Are sneakers required for gym and, if so, can they safely be kept in school? Ask what type of clothing the students usually wear. Find out where and when the school bus stops and where the crossing guards are stationed.

See if the school has a handbook for parents and students. These handbooks provide helpful information on school policies, curriculum, discipline procedures. Go over the handbook in detail with your child before school starts.

Take a tour of the building. It's helpful for a child to have a general idea of the layout of the school ahead of time. Find the bathrooms, library, cafeteria, gym. Older kids don't like to ask questions and show that they don't know something, so knowing the location of these areas ahead of time is important to them.

Let a younger child play on the playground for a few minutes. A visit inside a classroom is also helpful. Sometimes it's even possible to meet the teacher ahead of time, which can be very reassuring for a young child. For older kids, who may have four or five different teachers during the day, meeting teachers ahead of time is not as important or feasible.

It's also helpful to find a neighborhood friend to go to school with on the first day. Encourage your child to establish one strong friendship in the new neighborhood before school begins. Invite a neighbor with kids the same age over for lunch one day and help foster the friendship. If you have trouble locating kids the same age, ask the secretary in the school office for a list of names of kids who live nearby.

Your attitude toward the new school will have an extremely strong influence on your child's ability to adjust to the situation. Don't have unrealistic expectations of how wonderful everything will be at first. Some things will go well, others won't. Allow your daughter to talk about what she likes or dislikes about this school, and what she preferred about her previous school. You might even encounter a few tears and recriminations such as, "You were so mean to move. I hate this awful school. I wish we had stayed where we were!" Your job is to listen to her and to support her, not to argue your daughter out of such feelings. Adjustment takes time, and her feelings will gradually change if you do not pressure her to like everything at once.

Don't run down the school or teachers in front of your daughter, or make unfavorable comparisons to the previous school. Do become active in the new school yourself. Join the PTA. If you have concerns or things you'd like to see changed in the school, talk to the principal or the PTA officers.

If you express interest and satisfaction in the new school, your daughter will most likely follow your example.

Travel Tips

Q. My husband's vacation this year does not occur at the same time as our three children's school vacation. We would like to take a family trip, which would mean that the kids would miss a whole week of school. Is it legal to keep kids out of school for a vacation? Even if it is, do you think it's a good idea, or will the kids miss too much at school?

A. Because the rules regarding compulsory attendance at school are set independently by each state, there are variations from state to state on how many days a student must attend school each year to pass and which absences are considered legal. Some states allow local districts to decide upon the legality of absences.

States also vary in their responses to illegal absences. In

some states the illegal absence is simply recorded on the student's permanent record. In others the student's family is fined. Fines are legal as long as the parents have been informed of the policy in advance, they can afford to pay the fine, and the children are not excluded from school if the fine hasn't been paid. Yet another response to illegal absences is to fail a child and force him to repeat a grade or certain subjects if his illegal absences reach a certain number. The legality of failing a child for absences is questionable.

You need to find out your district's policy. Many districts have a handbook containing this information. If yours doesn't, call either the school principal or superintendent's office. Don't be surprised if you get different responses from the principals of different schools. Senior high schools often aren't as flexible as elementary schools regarding absences.

Aside from the question of legality, a family trip can be every bit as educational for your children as a week in the classroom. A trip is a wonderful opportunity to learn more about the geography and history of a new area. Kids can practice their reading skills by reading books about the area. Math skills can be practiced if kids are allowed to compute mileage or keep track of expenses. The children's teachers can give you more specific suggestions on how to make your trip educational for your children.

About two weeks before the trip is to begin, set up a conference between you, your children, and their teachers so your child doesn't fall behind during a trip. Find out what work will be missed and get the assignments ahead of time. Try to arrange for your child to do these assignments before the vacation, since it's hard to do schoolwork while on a trip. Use the actual vacation time to concentrate on the educational aspects of the trip itself, an experience that can't be duplicated in school. Also make arrangements ahead of time for each of your children to meet with a classmate as soon as you return. The classmate can fill each kid in on what happened when he or she was away.

By consulting with your children's teachers ahead of time you avoid the bad feelings that are generated when parents just take their kids out of school without a word. When teachers and parents plan together, family trips can become an exciting educational experience.

Asking for the Teacher You Want

Q. What do you think about the idea of parents requesting a specific teacher for their child? Because our older son had a fourth grade teacher who did wonders for him, we'd like our daughter to have the same teacher. Is it unrealistic to think the school would honor such a request?

A. Proponents of parent involvement in the schools encourage parents to make such requests. They feel that parents deserve some control over their kids' education, and choosing a teacher is one way to exercise that control. Because your family has had such a positive experience with this teacher, most likely your daughter would fare well with her also. Positive expectations on both sides, the child's and the teacher's, is known to greatly benefit school performance.

Such parental requests, however, can cause difficulties for the school. When too many parents choose one teacher and another teacher has no such requests, it may create popularity contests. Teachers fear they'll be caught in a situation that could damage school morale. A teacher who is not requested might not necessarily be incompetent, either. Indeed, a teacher could become unpopular just by setting higher standards and requiring more work, even though the standards and the work were in the students' best interests.

Most school administrators attempt to set up balanced classes. They may mix classes by achievement levels, race, sex, and socioeconomic levels. If they honored all parents' requests, lopsided class balances might result. Yet if they honor some parents' requests and not others, angry parents may be knocking on their doors.

Thus your quite legitimate desire to request a specific teacher conflicts with the school's need to balance classes and protect staff morale. Some schools have found a delicate solution. While they allow, and honor, requests wherever possible, at the same time they ask parents to understand the issues involved and to avoid angry protests when a request cannot be fulfilled. When cooperation and support reflects the behavior of both the school and the home, the kids become the ultimate winners.

Sports, Sports, and More Sports

Q. My thirteen-year-old son spends most of his time after school involved in one sport or another. By the time he gets home, showers, and eats dinner, it's often late and he's too tired to do his homework. His low grades are reflecting his lack of studying. Should I make him stop all sports until his grades improve?

A. I doubt that forbidding sports or even threatening to forbid sports will accomplish your goal. Most likely such action will generate hostility in his relationship with you. Deprived of what he loves best, your son is likely to get defiant and stubborn. In such a battle of wills, everyone loses.

Don't downgrade the value of athletic programs for youngsters. Undoubtedly your son feels a sense of belonging and a sense of accomplishment from his participation. Sports allow him to keep physically fit. Playing on a team provides opportunities for building friendships and requires him to think and use his judgment as he makes split-second decisions on the field. Finally, physical activity and competition provides an emotional release from tensions that build up during the day.

Your role is to encourage and help him plan his time so

that studies are not neglected. You want to tell him that it is OK to participate in sports, but he must find a way to study, too. Point out how many athletes are also musicians or artists or actors—noting that they do not limit themselves to just one thing. At thirteen, he should not be limiting himself either. Encourage outside interests in reading, music, or the theater by inviting him to join you as you participate in these activities.

Your son may need to try a number of different plans before he decides on a satisfactory way to participate in sports and study effectively, too. Remain supportive by expressing your approval of his athletic interests; at the same time affirm the need for good study habits and improved grades. As he tries out plans other than the ones you might suggest, remain flexible. He is learning a valuable lesson in how to plan his time to meet his needs and commitments. Learning this skill now will be of great benefit to him in the future.

Soliciting Funds on Fund Drives

Q. Frequently school organizations sponsor fund drives to buy items for the school that are not included in the regular budget. These efforts usually mean my kids are knocking on doors selling cards or candy or tickets to some event. Is teaching kids to solicit really such a good idea?

A. Fund-raising is a fact of life for most organizations. Schools, churches, scouts, and charities all supplement budgeted funds by selling and soliciting contributions. As federal, state, and local funds dry up, fund-raising activities by non-profit organizations, including schools, probably will increase.

Few children have money of their own that they can contribute to their school. But most children do have spare time that they can contribute instead. By asking children to contribute, we boost their sense of belonging and of being an important part of the school community. Too often kids are just the product of schools and have no active part in planning or operating them. By raising funds, and having a limited say in how the funds are spent, they become partners with teachers and parents in their own education. The more involved the kids feel, the greater their sense of commitment and pride in their school.

Most school fund-raising activities are initiated by a parents' group. These activities should be joint activities by parents, staff, and kids. Kids should not be doing just the leg work; they should have input into setting up the fund drive and deciding how the money will be spent. The actual selling activities should also be a joint adult-child activity. Before the selling begins, kids and their parents should sit down together and discuss plans for where, when, and how to sell.

Parents could even role-play how to talk to a customer, stressing politeness and courtesy on the seller's part. No person should be pressured into buying, regardless of how worthy the cause is. Stay interested in how your children proceed with their fund-raising activities, but do not relieve them of the responsibility for living up to their commitments by selling their shares yourself. Remember, this is a joint activity. You carry out your commitment to sell; they must carry out theirs. Be supportive, answer questions, praise their accomplishments, but leave their leg work to them. It's their decision how hard to work and how much to sell.

Appendix 1
••••••••••••••••••••••••••••••••

Recommended Reading

Albert, Linda. *Linda Albert's Advice for Coping with Kids*. New York: E. P. Dutton, Inc., 1982.

Corsini, Raymond, and Painter, Genevieve. *The Practical Parent*. New York: Harper and Row, 1975.

Dinkmeyer, Don, and McKay, Gary. *Raising a Responsible Child*. New York: Simon and Schuster, 1973.

————. *The Parent's Handbook: Systematic Training for Effective Parenting*. Circle Pines, MN: American Guidance Service, 1982.

————. *The Parent's Guide: Systematic Training for Effective Parenting of Teens*. Circle Pines, MN: American Guidance Service, 1983.

Dreikurs, Rudolph, and Soltz, Vicki. *Children: The Challenge*. New York: E. P. Dutton, Inc., 1964.

Appendix 2

••••••••••••••••••••••••••••••••••

Recommended Parent–Training Programs

Systematic Training for Effective Parenting, American Guidance Service, Circle Pines, MN 55014

Systematic Training for Effective Parenting of Teens, American Guidance Service, Circle Pines, MN 55014

Active Parenting, Active Parenting, Inc., 2996 Grandview Ave., Suite 312, Atlanta, GA 30305

For information on parent-training programs in your area, contact local schools, churches, family-service agencies, or mental-health centers.

Appendix 3

• •

Resource Organizations for Parents

Association for Children with Learning Disabilities, 4156 Library Rd., Pittsburgh, PA 15234

Children's Defense Fund, 122 C Street N.W., Washington, D.C. 20001

Council for Basic Education, 725 15th St. N.W., Washington, D.C. 20005

Council for Exceptional Children, 1920 Association Dr., Reston, VA 22091

The Home and School Institute, 1201 16th Street N.W., Washington, D.C. 20001

National Association for Gifted Children, 2070 County Rd. H., St. Paul, MN 55112

National Committee for Citizens in Education, 410 Wilde Lake Village Green, Columbia, MD 21044

National School Volunteer Program, 300 N. Washington St., Alexandria, VA 22314

National PTA, 700 N. Rush St., Chicago, IL 60611

Index

DATE DUE

	LOS BANOS		
	JUL 22 1986		